ALSO BY

JONATHAN LITTMAN

THE WATCHMAN

"Jonathan Littman's account of Kevin Poulsen…reads like a cat-and-mouse-with-keyboards thriller. *The Watchman* is a guided tour through the subculture of "phreaks" — hackers obsessed with tapping into the telephone company…his use of present-tense narrative gives one the feeling of looking over the shoulder as he hacks and hatches his schemes."

—*New York Times Book Review*

THE FUGITIVE GAME

"The Fugitive Game stands alone. Jonathan Littman has written the inside scoop, intricately depicting the life of the cybercriminal on the run. His revelations…are astonishing."

—*Christian Science Monitor*

THE ART OF INNOVATION

WITH TOM KELLEY

"On nearly every page, the story of some upstart invention is recounted in patter that's as good as a skilled magician's… Almost like visiting an IDEO workshop in person." —*Wired*

THE TEN FACES OF INNOVATION
WITH TOM KELLEY

"The Ten Faces of Innovation superbly maps how people and processes can be managed to innovate successfully. It makes explicit the intuition and experience of the world's master innovator. Every business executive should read it."
—Clayton Christensen, Harvard Business School

THE BEAUTIFUL GAME

"This is a story that should be passed along, girl to girl, mother to mother, dad to dad." —*USA Today*

I HATE PEOPLE!
WITH MARC HERSHON

"I Hate People" is a bracing antidote to the management bromide that "there is no 'i' in 'team.'" —*Wall Street Journal*

ONCE UPON A TIME IN COMPUTERLAND

"An exciting story well told." —James Michaels, *Forbes*

CRASHING
AUGUSTA

REAL LIFE TALES
OF SPORTS,
MEN, AND MURDER

Jonathan Littman

SNOWBALL
NARRATIVE

MILL VALLEY, CALIFORNIA

Snowball Narrative
38 Miller Ave. Suite 122
Mill Valley, CA 94941
Visit our website at www.snowballnarrative.com

First Edition: November 2010

Cover design by Bryan Haker

Stories previously published in *Playboy*

Library of Congress Cataloging-in-Publication Data

Littman, Jonathan.
  Crashing Augusta, real life tales of sports, men and murder/
Jonathan Littman.
  p. cm.
Previously published in Playboy.
1. Sports. 2. Golf. 3. Football. 3. Baseball. 4. Running. 5. Hazing. I. Title

ISBN: 1453693440
ISBN-13: 9781453693445
Library of Congress Control Number 2010910763

Printed in the United States of America

FOR LIZ, KATE
AND SHERRY

CONTENTS

CRASHING AUGUSTA

INTRODUCTION

In the spring of 2003, I got a call from a state narcotics agent whose crime fighting exploits I had recently chronicled. Iran White had stunning news: He was now working undercover on a steroids case in Barry Bonds' gym just south of San Francisco. In the months and years that followed I would write two *Playboy* stories and dozens more for other publications on BALCO, the biggest investigation of sports doping in history.

I learned that leads can come from anywhere and how sometimes one story will take you to another. At a Christmas party, I met a hedge fund manager who told me a fascinating story of how he'd put himself through college hustling football and basketball tickets. He had two colorful brothers who had followed in his footsteps and were still deeply entrenched in the mysterious world of ticket hustling. That February I hopped a plane cross-country, and for one crazed, Hunter Thompson-esque week, I travelled with the brothers to the Super Bowl, carried a leather satchel with a quarter of a million dollars in tickets and cash, and experienced the raw and dangerous world of big time sports ticket hustling first hand.

That Super Bowl piece led me to Augusta National and the fabled Masters. I decided to start by first phoning Bob Young, the Mayor of Augusta, and he kindly gave me the journalist's equivalent of the key to city: Introductions to every major character in the home of golf's greatest tournament, including the Sheriff. For someone who has had a life-long love affair with golf this was better than a vacation. Spending a week at The Masters peeling back the tournament's rich history and beautifully conflicted Southern traditions, all the while taking in the glorious golf course and watching the game's greatest players, was a duffer's dream.

It's no secret that the Internet and economic forces have put the world of books and narrative magazine writing under siege. Several years ago, I was lucky to become a Contributing Editor at *Playboy*. While books have always been the mainstay of my writing, this unusual but venerable magazine offered me a wonderfully diverse range of subjects.

Playboy was one of the few publications in America that celebrated narrative driven stories that sometimes seemed too wild to be true, stories that proved the old axiom, "Truth is stranger than fiction." While the slippery edge of professional sports was my beat, my gifted Playboy editors, Chris Napolitano, Bob Love and A.J. Baime, had open minds. If I could find a tale men would care about, all I had to do was find a way to tell the story.

One evening I heard a radio interview about a young man murdered on campus in a rite of manhood gone horribly awry. Within days, I was on campus and then in the office of the local District Attorney who brought criminal charges. It wasn't long before I was face to face with the men in prison togs who killed Matt Carrington. That story touched me in a way few do. Matt was a bright, young man who deserved a future. While two of the stories in this collection won awards, I will never forget *The Basement*. When the story came out, *Playboy* sent a copy to Governor Arnold Schwarzenegger. Soon after, he signed *Matt's Law*, and for the first time in California, the perpetrators of deadly hazing rites could be charged with felonies.

In the whimsical tradition of George Plimpton, whenever possible, I have taken the opportunity to slip into worlds that my talents wouldn't normally grant me access. Every fan has at one time or another wondered what it would be like to line up next to a professional athlete. I've always loved sports, and played college soccer, and once was reasonably quick. Nearing 50, I tracked down some of the fastest men in the world, Maurice Greene, and Jeremy Wariner, and tagged along for sprint workouts. Yes, it was a story, but I can't say that was my primary motivation. I'll never forget the experience of running with the world's fastest 400-meter runner through a graveyard in Waco, Texas, or performing sprint drills on a West Los Angeles track with a dozen of the world's fastest men and women.

Life is about surprises, those human twists and turns that you'd never expect. I invite you to spend a week at The Masters or the Super Bowl, peer behind the scenes of the world's biggest investigation of sports doping, and perhaps even descend to the dank basement where a young man was murdered.

I can promise you that you'll never look at these worlds in the same way again.

TICKETS

The Men Who Can Get You
Into the Super Bowl

*"Most of the time, they won't even know
who you are. I might even say you're the bagman."*

— THE LITTLE GENERAL

THE TICKET MASTERS

The black Dodge Ram weaves through traffic at 85 miles an hour like a tailback following a block. Destination: Jacksonville, Florida. The Little General taps his can of Skoal against the steering wheel, a silver Rolex glinting on his wrist. Junior, in faded jeans, mirrored shades, his blond hair cropped with a wave, rides shotgun.

"Hello Moto! Hello Moto!" their phones chirp in unison. The brothers do a double take and burst out laughing. They haven't seen each other in a while and can't believe they've picked the same ring for their brand spanking new cells. Which makes it kind of silly since their $700 Razrs ring practically on the minute.

Crammed in back are three big suitcases, jackets, shirts and two leather shoulder bags with $165,000 in cash and another $70,000 in tickets. No guns. At least none I've been told about.

It's Wednesday afternoon of Super Bowl week. The brothers are ticket brokers, hustlers. This is the first leg of their Triple Crown—the Super Bowl, followed by college basketball's Final Four, and the Masters. You want to be there, they deliver the ticket. Every experience has its price, and the final price of this experience is constantly in flux. Wireless notepad open on his lap, Junior scans ticket prices on TraderDaily.com. Prices seem to be creeping up, but then again he isn't sure the numbers are real—yet. It's a futures exchange. As in the stock market or the Chicago exchange, you can make a killing or get killed. In past years the brothers have made out handsomely on the world's biggest football game. Four out of five Super Bowls, they raked it in. But the older brother, the Little General in this operation, has no idea how this one will turn out. He has ample orders for seats priced from $1,800 to $2,300, paid in advance with credit cards and corporate checks by some of his best clients. The $165,000 in cash is to buy the tickets in Jacksonville from fellow brokers and hustlers. "We're in a little trouble on the get-ins," he explained the night before about the lowest-priced seats. "Our cream orders should be fine. Those prices are coming down." It's all a calculated gamble. His main hedge is that he has insisted on late delivery times—mostly Saturday and

Sunday—which give him a little more leeway to turn a profit.

There are other risks. As we near Jacksonville, the General takes a call from a broker who sent a runner there to "dig tickets." The runner—and the cash—have gone missing.

"How much cash did he have?" probes the General. "Six figures?"

"Almost."

"Did you check the police and hospitals?"

"Yeah."

"All right. If you need us to do anything, let us know. We'll keep our fingers crossed."

The General hangs up. "I hate bad stories," he says. "That's a bad story."

"That's a very scary story," Junior says. "Maybe he's got a gambling problem."

"Or someone could of rolled him," says the General, spitting in his cup.

The brothers fall silent on that thought. It's too late in the day to squirrel their $165,000 in a Jacksonville safe deposit box. And tonight, with hordes of thieves, hookers, gangsters, pickpockets, and all manner of con artists descending on this backwater city for our nation's biggest sports extravaganza, we're not exactly staying at Fort Knox. It's February 2, day one of the Super Bowl ticket hustle. The brothers need to buy and deliver about 110 tickets. The countdown begins; kickoff is in just four days.

I first meet the Little General in the bedlam of his hometown NBA team's coliseum after a victory at the buzzer. The Little General is not tall. Although he hails from the Midwest, he has a Southern patrician demeanor about him, and he's square-jawed with bright eyes and a broad grin. Junior is the head turner in the family, with a natural lip snarl, a wicked sense of humor, and an ease that recalls a young Paul Newman. I know the duo's other brother, a hedge-fund manager who lives thousands of miles away. At a Christmas party the eldest brother told me how he'd grown up scalping tickets—and how both his younger brothers followed in his footsteps and never tired of the hustle. And why would they? Brokers at the General's level make $300,000 to $500,000 a year, largely by buying in advance and then reselling blocks of tickets for NBA and college football games. That is their day job, one that leaves ample time for leisure or the vice of their choice. The Super Bowl is where they throw the dice, making or losing as much as $80,000 in a single week.

The Little General is a man who lives by his cell phone, so in the middle of our first few phone conversations he would drop off to do tickets. Once, after an unusually long interruption he came back on the line. "That was kind of a weird one," he said. He'd just completed the sale of two tickets to Bush's inaugural ball (a friend is buddies with a congressman). Then again, I once called the General on a weekday morning, and he asked me to hold on; I heard muffled voices and then, "Get up, get up, get up—*get in the hole!*" The General's daytime office is his golf club. Except for five madcap days at the Super Bowl and the whirlwind, back-to-back weeks of the Final Four and the Masters, the General mostly works on his swing.

The night of my arrival at the NBA coliseum, we have spoken for just a few minutes when he invites me to join him at his Tuesday-night poker game. On the way out he shares a kiss with the cute waitress. His new Ram truck is parked out front, a stone's throw from the arena. We cruise a residential neighborhood and the site of tonight's game might as well have a neon sign on it—two lipstick-red doors with portholes that look as if they were torn from a nightclub. Inside, I find a felt-covered poker table crowded by eight raucous men. A girl bursting out of her bikini top gives the General his first shot of vodka—with her cleavage. She lowers her breasts to serve up my first refreshment too.

"I was afraid you might be a bookworm," the Little General says and smiles. "You'll be fine."

The General offers a preview of some of the characters we'll be meeting in the next few days. "Most of the time, they won't even know who you are," he says. "I might even say you're the bagman."

THE DEAL

The General is considered a midsize, licensed broker. He takes far more risk than smaller brokers who lack the resources or constitution to take dozens or hundreds of advance orders for major events like the Super Bowl or Final Four. The General's clients are salesmen, businessmen, lawyers and major corporations. His tickets come from some of those same clients as well as a network of street hustlers and scalpers. In the food chain above the General sit the major national brokers with revenues ranging from tens of millions of dollars to $100 million, firms like RazorGator Tickets, Encore Tickets and TicketCity. Recently, TicketsNow and StubHub have emerged as big online players.

Some Super Bowl facts: the NFL presold more than 78,000 tickets to the game, though it does not want to say exactly how many or precisely to whom. "It's a private business," says Brian McCarthy of the NFL. "It's not a secretive thing. It's just a business practice."

The NFL sells 13,000 tickets at $600 each and approximately 65,000 at $500, adding up to ticket sales of more than $40 million. If the Super Bowl was a dud, that would be the end of it. But of course it's a massively popular spectacle. Tens of thousands of the some 78,000 tickets are resold through brokers and scalpers to corporations and individuals. The NFL says it "really has no idea" how many tickets are resold, though it eagerly acknowledges that "tickets sold at $500 or $600 are probably woefully underpriced."

Upon winning the AFC Championship in Pittsburgh, the Patriots took possession of 17.5 percent of the Super Bowl tickets, which are held by the NFL in a vault. The math confused me at first. The NFL states that "no tickets are given away. Everyone pays for them." That means owners, players, corporations, and fans. So on January 23, or soon after, the Patriots had to pay the NFL for nearly 14,000 tickets—in other words, the team coughed up more than $7 million.

That sounds like a $7 million penalty for making it to the Super Bowl, unless you dig a little deeper. Two thousand tickets would easily take care of each team's players and staff, as well as a number of bigwigs. What do the teams do with their other 12,000 tickets? Neither the Patriots nor the Eagles would comment. Nor would any of the other major entities who pay for NFL ticket allotments—Budweiser, Fox, CBS and Ford. Typical was the response of a Pepsi-Cola spokeswoman: "We don't share information about when we receive tickets and how many we receive."

Despite the official silence, the brokers I interviewed estimate that roughly 25 percent of the allotments—nearly 25,000 tickets—enter what's called the secondary market. The opening market price for those tickets ranged from $1,900 to $6,000. If you take an average final resale range of $2,500 to $2,600, you come up with a $2,000 average markup. Multiply that by 25,000 tickets and you get $50 million in profit for those who sell and resell those secondary tickets. That's an estimate of how much NFL teams, players, sponsors, brokers, scalpers, and fans can make on the difference between a ticket's face value and its street value. In other words, the lucky souls who get NFL allotments—the chance to pay $500 to $600 for strips of cardboard—can easily triple or quadruple their money.

Who gets the tickets depends on who you are. As George Orwell wrote in *Animal Farm*, "All animals are equal, but some animals are more equal than others." When it comes to the Super Bowl, the most equal animals are the owners of the two participating teams, who receive a combined 35 percent. The host city's team gets five percent, and the networks, official sponsors, and charities combined receive more than 24 percent. The 29 other teams in the league each receive a scant 1.2 percent. Active players—the workhorses—get two tickets each. Super Bowl players get the option to buy another 15 tickets. Fans don't receive a single straight allotment. The 30,000 of them who mailed postcards to the NFL were entered into a drawing for 500 winners (two tickets per winner), a one-in-60 chance to buy tickets. The Eagles and Patriots both say their season ticket holders were entered in certified drawings to buy some portion of their tickets. Neither would disclose how many tickets fans got the chance to buy.

TICKET SCALPING

The NFL's clandestine method of distributing Super Bowl tickets practically invites team owners, sponsors, advertisers, broadcasters, and players to resell their tickets at grossly marked-up prices, an annual reward for being an NFL partner, and a kind of insider stock deal. Officially, the NFL says it "doesn't have much of a view" on the difference between the tickets' face and street values. Nor does the NFL "give any specific instructions when it delivers the tickets. There wouldn't necessarily need to be." But league policy reminds teams and players that scalping is unethical and, in some states, illegal. "Scalping suggests a desire to profit personally and perhaps illicitly on the coattails of the league's popularity. Such conduct will not be tolerated," states the policy, which adds that scalping "may result in disciplinary action against the violator"—may being the operative word, though Minnesota Vikings head coach Mike Tice was tagged with a $100,000 fine when he admitted to selling some of his 12-ticket allotment for $1,900 apiece.

Any corporation that resells tickets must account for the revenue as income. Legitimate resales at original pricing are fine. Scalping is a gray area. Though legal in many states, it clearly contravenes NFL policy. Unreported cash transactions for any team or corporation that regularly receives NFL ticket allotments would be another matter. The threshold for federal prosecution, says the IRS, is proof that "the suspects did it as a continuing enterprise."

The NFL, the Super Bowl teams, and other major corporations know there is a huge resale market for the tickets. If an event has a perceived scarcity of tickets, engineered or not, prices soar. Anti-trust laws were designed to prohibit such anti-consumer activity—price-fixing. When two or more major players hold products off the market, that is called a conspiracy.

THE HUSTLE

The brothers' Razr phones ring 30 times or more in the half hour after we pick up Junior at the airport. The calls have a wonderful brevity and directness.

"Yeah, how much are they?"

"I'll take the six."

"You think the get-ins are going back up?"

"What's the weather forecast for the game?"

"You're done Tom, you don't have to call me every day. You're a 1,000 percent done."

"Casey wants to know—you want a four-pack for two dimes each?"

"There seems to be a little bit of a spike here."

Gliding on the cacophony of cell phone calls, we sweep in over the grey St. John's River on a wet, miserable afternoon. There's a cruise ship below, and ahead looms Alltel Stadium.

Five minutes later the General pulls up outside NFL headquarters, the Adam's Mark hotel. I clamber after quick-stepping Junior. In the packed bar, he greets John the Mormon. Baby-faced, wearing white Dockers, a banana-colored shirt and a brown suede jacket, he looks every bit the high school nerd. The Mormon and Junior start trading tickets and thousands in cash on the table like boys swapping baseball cards, while a couple of large black men at the bar raise their eyes at the spectacle. Trotting back to the car, Junior explains what went down. John the Mormon had a client with a bad pair of seats who wanted the best in the house. Junior knew where he could get his hands on a great pair. So John the Mormon's client said he'd give him $4,000 if he turned his bad ones into great ones. "John and I sat down and figured that if we lay out $6,500 to buy the two 50-yard-line tickets and our guy gives us $4,000—we're into our two seats for 25," explains Junior, meaning the deal so far has them $2,500 out of pocket. But then he says, "We sold the bad seats for $2,450 each and split $2,400 profit." That's ticket hustling.

Minutes later the General, who has an internal compass, has found the latest FedEx drop-off. Many deals are contingent on extremely tight deadlines, and the brothers wouldn't trust the U.S. mail in a million years. It's 7:15 p.m., a good 15 minutes before the cutoff, and we're parked in front of the purple-and-orange logo. Junior has half a dozen orders he's readying to go out for morning delivery. He's matching tickets to neatly printed air bills, making sure he has them straight. What's amazing is the faith and nonchalance. If a package is lost or gets sent to the wrong address, $10,000 or more of tickets turns into worthless cardboard. And get this: at 7:27 Junior doesn't even take the air pouches in himself. He talks a street scalper into walking his $40,000 worth of tickets into FedEx.

Hustlers and brokers saunter up to the General and Junior, knocking fists, trashing Jacksonville, and asking what the market is doing. A bald guy in a Super Bowl jacket hops in back, just the cash separating us.

"Four guys are missing right now," says the bald guy, "like they got kidnapped or something."

The General tells him he knows about one. "Who else?"

The bald guy mentions a Denver hustler and two others he doesn't know by name.

"Maybe the cops are grabbing people," says Junior.

"How did you hear about the other ones?" asks the General.

"The kid from Denver owes me money," says the bald guy. "He was the first one to go off the board, so I thought maybe he ran off with my money. Then there's another guy. Then they were talking two other guys from Chicago."

And just like that talk turns to where to eat. Fortunately, a call comes in from a guy I'll call Old Boy, who for the past few weeks has been telling the General he'll need a couple hundred tickets for his major corporate clients but has so far failed to deliver the cash. We're directed to an upscale Italian joint. The fish is light and buttery, the $150 chardonnay smooth as silk. The owner won't take our money.

A couple of hours later the General is not happy. A fellow broker sold him a few nights in a Motel 6 that the General figured he'd flip to customers, but one thing led to another.

"This is a disaster," says the General. Paint is chipping off the walls; the bed is a sponge. Ten minutes after checking in, I'm rapping on the brothers' door. The General answers in his boxers, $165,000 arrayed on the bed in neat stacks. The brothers are trying to "fix their start"—calculate how much they each put into the kitty so that sometime next week they can sort out exactly what they made or lost. Forget about how easy it would be to break the door or smash the window. They don't seem to have the least concern.

The Little General circles to the bathroom and pops out with a question. "Did you bring any shampoo?"

Junior deadpans, "No. I thought we were staying in a hotel."

Chuckling, the General holds up something only slightly thicker than a credit card. "Look, they gave us a bar of soap."

The General has been arrested seven times. He considers it mainly an inconvenience and a relatively infrequent one considering he's been doing this for more than 15 years. The General can't fathom why ticket scalping—reselling a ticket for substantially more than its list price—is illegal in many states. Here in Florida the charge is a second-degree misdemeanor with a fine of $75 to $200. A ticket friend bails him out, his attorney sends a check to a charity, and he shows up on the court date with his attorney to make certain the case is thrown out. The General says he's never been convicted.

Compare this with airlines, he says. American, Delta and United charge different prices at different times, as anyone gouged for a flight on short notice knows. Nobody charges American Airlines with scalping billions every year. Corporate insiders, meanwhile, receive stock for a dollar, flipping it out to the public at $20 in a public offering—a 1,900 percent markup. And what is a Wall

Street firm but suits scalping billions of dollars in stock? There's the futures exchange, where you can make or lose money betting on everything from pork bellies to the price of oil. Without people willing to bet on fledgling companies and the price of tomorrow's commodities, our modern economy would not exist.

TicketsNow, eBay, StubHub, and RazorGator think it's perfectly fine to resell tickets through auctions, online aggregations or listings. Online and auction sales are growing by leaps and bounds. Major League Baseball recently acquired Tickets.com, a move that despite official denials appears designed to offer secondary ticket marketing to the league's 30 teams, including those with anti-scalping policies. Business experts have heralded the increasing importance of the experience economy, and few modern experiences are more precious than attending celebrated sporting events like the Super Bowl or the Final Four. The idea that the price for such events can be set in stone a year or months in advance will soon be considered an anachronism.

THURSDAY

The Little General and I sit patiently in a downtown bank with $126,000 in cash in his leather shoulder bag. A grandmotherly black woman, first name Emma, brightens when the General hands over his account number, license, and black Amex. She pauses, smiling across the desk, "What pretty eyes you have," she says.

"Why thank you," says the General.

Emma walks us into the vault. The General pulls out box 382, and we walk into one of the private rooms, locking it behind us. He draws out the money from his bag. He counts the $10,000 bricks and the six slim ones and begins squeezing them into the 18-inch-long box. It's tight. Then it's back to the vault to be signed out. "Thanks, Emma."

The mood is light; it's been a day of boisterous greetings at the Adam's Mark, the centerpiece Super Bowl hotel, which by virtue of its designation as NFL headquarters has assumed the role of this week's de facto futures exchange. Perched on the bank of the meandering St. John's River, the hotel offers a colorful public stage. Docked across from the red-carpeted lobby entrance is a private yacht and one of the many cruise ships in town to provide extra rooms for the more than 100,000 visitors. Palm trees and a generous promenade line the river. The hotel is spacious and convivial, if less than elegant. A row of ferns separates the lobby from the sprawling dining room and adjoining bar, and a bustling souvenir stand butts up against a grand escalator that rises to the second floor, where ESPN broadcasts its radio show. Over the next 100 hours, the wheeling and dealing for Super Bowl tickets will be concentrated in three contiguous spots, from a dozen deal-makers' tables in the dining room and bar, to the lobby and the palm-lined port cochere.

As the General passes through the bar, he knocks knuckles with a dude built like a lineman, who says, "Hey, brother, you heard three guys got nabbed? You betta stow that shit."

The Little General doesn't miss a step, motioning to me, the guy in black leather and shades. "I got my muscle."

The General's first full day in Jacksonville begins as a reunion. Over the next increasingly tense four days, the General's club will comprise ticket guys and hustlers hailing from Massachusetts, Illinois, New Jersey, New York, Michigan, Minnesota, Texas, Kentucky, Georgia, North Carolina and Europe. Indeed the hotel has the feel of a hustlers' sales convention. The General's table resembles a men's club; women don't practice this hustle. Salty, affectionate nicknames are part of the culture of hustling, and except where noted, these terms of endearments are genuine (Because of the controversial legality of ticket hustling, my access was granted under the condition that no real names or home cities be identified).

The General's mentor is Sunshine, a bittersweet pit bull of a broker from the Midwest with one milky eye, who taught the General and his brothers to scalp in high school. Then there's Dirty, Sunshine's dogged Sancho Panza—a scruffy-looking clean freak—and also an Irishman we'll call Danny Boy, a tall ladies' man with a jaunty step, who, as the General says, "likes a bit of the drink." There's the aforementioned John the Mormon, as well as a sharp-eyed fellow we'll call Tex, who has the expression of a wise guy holding cards in a Sopranos poker game. Anonymous shall remain the beloved, nattily dressed 60-something Southern gentleman who appears to be a woman. For foreign events like soccer's Euro and World Cups, the General often partners with a freewheeling European we'll call Noodle. The General is one of many brokers who work the Super Bowl with a partner for practicality and camaraderie. Though the General confesses he sometimes thinks Junior is a bit too "loosey goosey," the risks he takes often make them big money. And two heads—and two pairs of arms and legs—can come in handy. The encroaching swirl of buys, sales, and deliveries, not to mention bank deposits and withdrawals, will soon demand that brokers be in three places at once.

Soon after the General sits, there's a commotion. Eagles cheerleaders prance down the escalator in their panty-like bottoms and slinky tops. The ticket guys barely glance up.

"What's going on?" says Tex. "How many guys are missing? I heard five."

"I heard one guy's missing with 175 grand," says another hustler.

Sunshine is disgusted. "I grew up with these guys, and I wouldn't give them that kinda money."

"From what I understand," explains another, "this one guy, he had a girl he'd do anything for."

Junior looks up from his laptop and smiles warmly. "Is there a finder's fee?"

One by one, bit players swing by the table with whispered entreaties, hustlers who dig tickets for the General and Junior. There's Tugboat who tops 450 pounds and swallows Junior up in a bear hug. Pie is a crusty six-foot-three New Englander with flaming hair and teeth like a jack-o'-lantern's; as the General so aptly puts it, Pie has no checking account, no Social Security number, a tax-free annual income nearing $100,000, and "a net worth of whatever happens to be in his pocket." Caveman has the protruding brow and squat build of our distant ancestors. The General has no illusions about the lowest rung, the scalpers and street hustlers who will soon infest every corner of the lobby. It's all the scalpers can do to remember the names of the brokers, often calling them by their home city, "Hey Miami!" or "Wassup, New York!" Big paydays like the Super

Bowl fuel the hustler sins—gambling, drugs, booze, and bad fashion. They can be spotted in windbreakers or pletherette jackets from past championships, caps, and sneakers. In the lobby the General points out a couple of Boston hustlers with head twitches, OxyContin addicts, and New Yorkers with hollow cheeks and haunted eyes, cokeheads.

Between greetings, the General mostly says no to offers to buy tickets, rarely acknowledging the hustler at his ear, almost never moving his eyes. He has the look of a man who has said no millions of times. Prices are up slightly this morning, and the General is waiting, a poker player calling the bluff. It's only Thursday; more than half the brokers won't even arrive till tomorrow. The General figures the national brokers who control untold thousands of seats are holding back supply to drive up early prices. "It's just ones and twos out there," he says of the tickets. "It's a Mexican standoff."

Sunshine leans back and offers up his lyrical interpretation: "Keyser Soze is just toying with us." In the film *The Usual Suspects*, Soze is a Merlin among thieves, a legendary, seemingly omnipotent master criminal who manipulates even the most hardened crooks behind the scenes. A few years back, at another Super Bowl, Sunshine stopped the General in the main hotel lobby and said, "There goes the Keyser Soze of the ticket business." The man inspires awe and fear. The ticket guys I meet this week wouldn't dare offer the Keyser's real name for publication. His reach is too far. Sunshine has heard that he controls about 7,000 of the some 25,000 secondary tickets available, and Sunshine knows that in this Darwinian game he is at best a small fish. When and how Soze releases thousands of seats will greatly sway the market.

No blinkers—counterfeits—for the game have been spotted, but Noodle has already been offered a sheet of six tickets to Playboy's party (note to counterfeiters: they aren't distributed to guests in sheets). So far, the cops are a minor distraction. Police posing as fans bust scalpers dumb enough to sell marked-up tickets to straights. Noodle's friend Smiley falls for a chick in the lobby who pays the bloated price of $3,000 for a single. Smiley hands her the ticket and she snaps on the cuffs. In the process, Noodle gets "heated up" by the cops. Before they can question him, the General approaches the other side of the row of greenery that separates the lobby from the dining room. Noodle executes a no-look-behind-the-back-pass, tossing the General a fistful of his business cards. "Hold on to these," he whispers, making certain the cops will find no evidence he's a broker.

"There's no reason to sell to a straight," says a bemused General. "Broker to broker it's very difficult to get arrested." In other words, stay in the club, buy from known hustlers and sell to known clients and you're unlikely to pay an unprofitable visit to a Jacksonville jail.

By evening, the General's band sets off for Thursday night's high-stakes poker game—the General at the wheel, Junior at his side, Sunshine, Dirty, and the writer in back. Junior's wife phones and asks for help with their son's fourth-grade homework and the hustlers warm to the task, whipping out calculators and shouting answers.

After stopping to load up on beer and Subway sandwiches, we drive to the dark outskirts of town. I can't say where. Who's there? Nobody. Nobody heats up the writer. Nobody says he's gonna have to look in my little leather notebook. Nobody doesn't like the word that I scratched down that I should have just kept in my head. Nobody says he's gonna have to search me for a wire, and Nobody does indeed pat me down. The General and Sunshine stick up for me, and Junior kindly tells a white lie in my defense. Things cool and the game gets rolling. Shortly after midnight Nobody shuffles up to me and says, "Let's go for a walk." We walk the grounds at a leisurely pace, and then I pull up abruptly at the gate to the pool. Nobody laughs. "Hey, relax. I ain't gonna snuff you." But Nobody isn't happy. "I can't figure you," he says. "You're smart. You don't talk. The whole sunglasses thing. Tell me what your story is gonna be?"

"It's Thursday," I say. "The game isn't till Sunday."

Nobody isn't happy. "The best story you could write about the ticket business," he says, "is no story."

Ticket hustling is risky business. The General has been threatened more than once by Knockout Pete, a sturdy Italian known to slam against walls those hustlers who fail to donate fast enough. In New York, the General once bought some prized Final Four tickets off a couple alumni—netting a quick $24,000 in profit he declined to share. Knockout banged on the General's getaway cab, shouting, "I'm gonna f---ing kill you if I see you again!"

The General has never been held up with a gun, though he has employed off duty cops to carry the bag at previous Super Bowls (Many ticket guys carry guns). Like any veteran broker or hustler, the General confesses to having tickets robbed "right from my hands."

You want to be a ticket broker? A hustler? Think again. Play at the General's level or above and there are pressures most couldn't stomach. At one Super Bowl the General had dozens of pre-orders at $2,000. Prices zoomed up to $3,000 and in a few days he lost $80,000 meeting his obligations to deliver his clients' seats.

The Masters is the last and perhaps most prestigious leg on the hustler's Triple Crown. Like the tournament, Masters hustling is very much an old boys network. Long ago, Augusta assigned lifetime Tournament or Series badges to club members and a select patron list. The annual fee for this privilege is just $175. Patrons caught reselling their badges can lose their annuity but the profits can be huge. Badge prices have ranged from $3,000 to more than $10,000, making some brokers rich on the upswing and breaking others.

As the General wheels out of the Motel 6 lot at eight a.m. sharp, Dirty announces he had a dream. Someone broke into his room. "They were trying to get all our money," he says. "I shot him in the leg twice."

The General spits in his plastic cup. "I gotta get money out."

Junior has checked online, and prices are up. So say the other brokers who've already called. "Look how smart that Keyser is," says Sunshine. "He tells the Patriots not to release their seats till Saturday."

The General will require a lot of cash to buy the 100 or so seats he still needs for his clients. The General and I get out at the bank, where we say hello to Emma and withdraw the entire $126,000, to go with the 25 grand he kept, which means the General is now walking the streets of Jacksonville with over $150,000 in cash.

At breakfast at the Adam's Mark, the General proposes a sit-down with another major broker to see if they can buy on credit. He's deployed that strategy before to counter spiraling prices: buy with the rising market, sell while it's high. Though it's still early—two and a half days till kick-off—there's no doubt about the upswing. The General has surveyed fellow brokers in the lobby, and everybody's buying. Lots of deliveries have to be made in the next few hours. Meanwhile he's been summoned upstairs. A kingpin broker has ordered the General "to bring him every ticket" he's got.

"People are starting to panic," says Junior, shaking his head as his brother walks off. Junior has deliveries that need to be made today. He's got to start buying faster—a pair of lower corners at 26 from Pie, meaning $2,600. That's $600 more each than they would have cost him three days before. "People are gonna lose a lot of money today," Sunshine says. "Keyser's not releasing his tickets. It's like trying to put your finger in the dyke."

Fifteen minutes later, the General returns with a fresh dilemma. Old Boy, a notoriously late payer, wants the General to supply him with just under half a million dollars' worth of tickets on credit. Sunshine surveys the

General and Junior. "You guys are crazy if you're even considering it," he says.

The General and Junior reach a compromise. They'll buy Old Boy as many seats as he gives them cash for, but they'll buy on credit only if he arranges a sit-down with the major corporations that are his ultimate clients and if they in turn sign a contract. For weeks, Old Boy has promised to wire the General a quarter million dollars or more to pay for the seats. Without the cash it's a huge gamble.

The Little General strides through the lobby, which is now packed with hustlers. By the palm tree across from the private yacht, just after a ticket delivery, something good happens. Tugboat is beached on the bench, when three Southern boys roll in. The General just knows. "Extras?" he says coolly.

"Yes," one man replies, pointing to his ruddy-faced friend talking on a cell. They stop. The General waits. The man clicks off.

"How many do you have?" asks the General.

"Six," he replies, giving their location.

"How much would you like?" asks the General pleasantly.

"Two," says the man.

"I've got bindles. Is that okay?" says the General, stepping over to open his leather bag on a concrete planter box, 40 feet from the valet. No time for second thoughts, he counts out $12,000 in exchange for six strips of orange cardboard. He turns and smiles. "I'll cut you in, Tugboat."

As the men walk off, Tugboat shuffles up. "A nickel would be good," he says, and the General hands him $500. As we stroll the promenade with Danny Boy, Junior, and Dirty to grab lunch, the General explains that technically he sliced Tugboat, cut into his turf. Hence the nickel. The General's mood has lifted. Minus Tugboat's $500 commission, he just bought six good tickets he can flip for a quick $6,000 profit. The count has ticked down to 94 seats.

Waiting for a table by the jam-packed ESPN outdoor TV stage, the General and Danny Boy spy a Saint Bernard dragging a man in a black leather jacket by a leash. The man's other hand is wrapped around a Bud.

"Got tickets?" the General asks.

The man's massive head swings like a bobble-head doll. He's dead drunk. Mirror shades make him look like a giant toy. He wags his enormous butt like his dog. The General motions to Danny Boy to move in for the close. They dance about the price.

"He'll sell," whispers the General. "He's a local."

"How do you know?" I stupidly ask.

"Saint Bernards don't travel well," says the General.

The man hands the leash to a friend and waddles off with Danny Boy. Five minutes later the Irishman saunters back. "Bumped him down from 25 to 23" he says. He hopped out of the chaos into the nearest clothing store. "I slipped the salesgirl a 20," Danny says. "I was in, I was out. Ninety-two hundred for the four."

Danny Boy and the General split the profits. But Junior's gotten a call: two New York hustlers with tickets to sell. Just like that I'm jogging through the crowd to keep up, the General spooked about the impending purchase. Junior is getting loosey goosey, and the General has seen these particular New Yorkers pound rival hustlers.

Junior spins in the middle of the traffic-snarled street. The General calmly strides up to the traffic cop, something north of $110,000 draped over his shoulder. "Ma'am, where's North Liberty?"

Junior grabs the bag and trots off down the sidewalk. Ahead, a hustler hangs on to the back door of a white compact and motions Junior in with a leering grin.

"Don't get in the car!" the General cries. "Don't get in the car!" But little brothers never listen. The door closes, and Junior is inside.

The General shakes his head as they drive off. "You don't get in a car with guys like that!" We're trotting around the corner after the car, the General on his cell, asking me, "Where did they go?"

Minutes later, the General looks up to find Junior on the street, unscathed and still in possession of the bag. After making certain his brother is all right, he takes a breath and says in front of the Adam's Mark, "Let's eat like civilized people."

The General gathers up his band and leads us into the more fashionable restaurant just off the lobby. Warren Moon sits two tables to our right. "If you want, you can put your bag over here," the helpful waitress says to the General, pointing to a chair by the window.

The gang howls. "Why don't you just put it outside, sir," Junior jokes. "Nobody will bother it."

The Little General rescues the befuddled waitress with a kind smile, patting the bag. "I think I'll just keep it right here."

He takes his natural position at the head of the long table. To his left, Danny Boy begins counting 100s. Two seats down, Junior looks as if he's playing solitaire, except the 30 cards are tickets, nearly $90,000 at this hour's prices—80 left to buy.

Sunshine leans in, surveying the seat numbers.

"Let's do some trades," he says.

"Whadda ya need?" says Junior.

The pimply busboy comes by to fill our water glasses and stands gaping. The tickets. The cash. "Could I just stand here?" he says.

Thirty feet away, out in the lobby, undercover cops are working to bust scalpers, yet in this sanctuary the Little General calmly orders the blackened grouper with a sweet tea, Dirty tucks into some bread, and Danny Boy orders pizza.

"Here's your 11 grand," Danny says, handing Junior a stack. "I owe you 100." Upon which Danny turns to the General and in a jovial tone starts talking about the upcoming U2 concert. "You wanna come to Dublin in June?" he asks. "We'll go over, work the show, blast it out."

But there's a dark undertow. Old Boy has crept in like a bad chill and drawn the General off to a nearby table, where they speak in hushed tones. Under the table he hands the General $26,000 in cash and $6,000 in a cashier's check and tells him two $25,000 wire transfers will be hitting his account any minute. The cash and cashier's check mean the General's ticket orders have just climbed back up about 10 tickets—90 to go. Then Old Boy gets up to leave and says in a toneless voice that he'll pick up the tab.

"I don't want your money," says Danny Boy, tossing a bill onto the table, shaking his head at Old Boy and slinging the classic hustler refrain, "Get stuck. Stay stuck." He's twisting the knife in a stuck broker's heart. Danny knows Old Boy needs tickets bad. And that knowledge means the price just went up.

SATURDAY

Jack Kemp—the former congressman, vice presidential candidate, and pro quarterback—calmly reads his paper 20 feet from the boys' table. It's Saturday breakfast at the Adam's Mark and the pressure is building. Only one of Old Boy's $25,000 wires hit the General's account. Junior has to deliver half his seats today. At current broker prices— about $3,000—they could lose $500 to $800 a ticket, but even so they have to accelerate the buying. By noon they still need 60, and the General is seeking evidence that prices are cooling. Danny Boy just told him he bought a pair at $3,200 each and had to dump them at $3,000 to get out of them—losing money. Says the General, "I take that as a good sign." It looks as though the market may be turning.

Star sightings are on the upswing. A once-celebrated quarterback watches Sunshine count out 30 grand near the hotel's safe deposit box, "That ain't chump change, Joe," Sunshine snorts at the ex-ballplayer.

Speaking of cash, the General's strapping lawyer buddy is carrying the bag. The Counselor's got the toughness and size of a defensive end. He's here for the action. "I like the spectacle of it," he says, motioning. "Look over there—it's Evander Holyfield." Sure enough, 20 feet away stands the boxer whose ear Mike Tyson chewed. The Counselor takes a strange pleasure in seeing his friends sweat. "Forty-eight weeks of the year these guys play golf and poker," he says, shaking his head. "I like to see them when they actually have to work.

"The money is insane," he says, the bag slung over his barrel chest. "Cash right out in the open. They don't even appreciate the danger." Just last night, he says, Junior saw someone in the lobby show excessive interest in the bag. "So he calls the General on his cell," says the Counselor. "Suddenly I'm the guy with the bag."

The Counselor says they treat money funny, and I couldn't agree more. Twenty-five feet away, dead center in the lobby, stands Sunshine, engulfed in scalpers and fans, pen tucked behind an ear, cell plastered to the other—tattered black briefcase carrying untold thousands cradled between his legs. Danny Boy rides the escalator above the fray, thumbing through 100s as he rises. Near the valet the General and Junior have turned a table into an impromptu bank, counting out thousands and exchanging tickets next to an oblivious TV camera crew filming fans.

It's carnival and street craps. Minutes later, next to the Bentley double-parked at the valet, Junior flips a coin with a hustler for the $200 they can't agree to on a pair of get-ins. The coin rolls nearly under the wheel. Heads. "The first flip he's won in two years," laughs the General.

A few minutes later the General is pacing. He's trying to fill the last two tickets of a nine-seat order for Junior. "I'm going to lose six grand on it," he says with a grimace. Two hours later, while washing down spaghetti and clams with the house red at a nearby Italian joint, the General explains, "For each order, there are five brokers bidding. You lose money. Or you bust the order—which I don't do."

This is the nasty downside of the advance order. The General has taken guaranteed contracts at just $2,300 per ticket, but the market Saturday evening has jumped to $3,500 a seat. They still need another 40. The General is losing $1,000 or more for every seat he buys. He's praying the market will fall. Maybe a big broker is holding back tickets and will need to unload them. Maybe he'll get lucky and pick up some packages off straights.

JONATHAN LITTMAN

"I'll remember what it feels like in my gut today," promises Sunshine. "That's why I don't give anybody a break. Ninety-five percent of the brokers are getting killed."

SUNDAY

At 10 a.m. in front of the seemingly deserted Adam's Mark, the General has run out of cash. It doesn't take a CPA to figure that every $3,000 they spend on a ticket now pushes them deeper into the red. A guy with a bowling ball in his shirt and a frog in his throat sidles up.

"You got any money?" asks Junior.

"Yeah."

"What can you give us?"

"Ten dimes."

Junior holds out his hand, and the guy plumbs his pocket and pulls out a wad the size of half a grilled cheese.

Junior doesn't count.

The guy with the belly turns to the General and smiles broadly. "I'm lending this to you, not him."

After days of rain and cold, Mother Nature conspires to drive up prices. The day breaks warm and clear—perfect Super Bowl weather. Squawking Eagles fans flap their wings through the crowd. A wife carries a sign, "Trade husband for tickets," while an expectant mom shows off the bulging-belly ad space she successfully bartered for two seats. But the best hustler I see all week is a steely Army recruiter. "If I give you a card to fill out would you?" the captain asks a couple of God-fearing youths.

"Would there be a commitment to join?"

"No, no commitment," says the captain, beaming.

Just 25 left. Every ticket is still selling for three dimes or more. The brothers snap out 100s with the cool efficiency of house card dealers. Old Boy desperately needs 150 more, but as the General notes, "he's about half a million dollars short."

A fellow broker offers the General a ticket at 35— $1,500 more than he could have bought it for a week ago. He passes.

Dirty walks up, disgusted. "The fans want $4,000 or $5,000 for their tickets."

"Tell 'em to get the fuck out of here!" snarls Sunshine.

Out front I talk to a bunch of Eagles fans. One got scammed paying $3,800 on eBay for a pair of tickets he never received. At 1:10, the General kneels behind the Bentley's back wheel, counting out cash he hands to a hustler for a pair. "It's coming down," he says. "We were being offered 35. Now it's 31. More tickets are coming out." With just five hours till kickoff, prices are finally falling.

Five minutes later the General stands before the lobby's revolving door, hustlers and fans streaming around him, voices roaring. He takes a small rubber band that a couple of hours ago was wrapped around a $10,000 brick and squeezes it around his forehead like a vise. He's already lost $20,000, and he still has to buy 20 more tickets. He feels like puking. Clients are pissed, wondering where their tickets are. He just wants to be done.

A hustler friend brushes by, adopting the tone of a hotel manager, "Sir, I believe you're wearing a rubber band on your head."

The General wades through the crowd to the red carpet out front. He looks as if he's going to bang his head against a steel post. "Next Super Bowl," he says. "Remind me that it will break at 1:15." Finally prices are falling—too late to do the General or Junior any good.

Time compresses. Lots of deliveries to Patriots and Eagles fans, even several Germans, part of the General's European clientele. The endgame approaches, and I take inventory. Sunshine, like virtually every medium-sized broker, lost tens of thousands. Danny Boy, a street hustler, made about $6,000. John the Mormon is one of the few modest-sized brokers who made good. He and his three partners made about $30,000 each. "We didn't take any orders; we're just flippin'," he says. He respects the General and Junior. "I couldn't do what they do. They're gamblers. Four out of five times it works. When it works, they make a lot of money."

It's 2:02. We're sitting out front on the ledge of a concrete planter. "You hold this, just stay here," the General says, leaving me the bag. "I'm going to confront Old Boy one last time in the Adam's Mark."

Super Bowl Sunday afternoon, and I'm left holding the bag, surrounded by hundreds of hustlers. After a couple of minutes I begin to relax. Nobody has time to notice me.

The General returns. Old Boy says the wires should be hitting his account. In the meantime he pleads again to buy half a million dollars' worth of tickets on credit. "I gotta find a plug for this," the General says, pointing to his dead cell phone. It's 2:30. Just inside the hotel side door, fighting the crowd, the General drops to his knees to plug in. There's no reception.

Up the escalator goes the General, and he turns the corner to plug in next to a column. Old Boy paces nearby but can't see us. The General gets a call from a customer three blocks away. "Walk in, go up the escalator and then turn to the right," he says. "He's in a black hat, black jacket, black glasses. Think man in black."

The General turns to me. "They've got two tickets. I gotta go downstairs and buy 'em. Give me five minutes."

He's reaching into the bag. "Where's that fucking rubber band? If I'd left it on my head, I'd have it now."

After scrounging, he finds another. "If Junior needs five grand, tell him it's the one with the rubber band around it." And then he's gone.

Three minutes later, two Patriots fans stroll up, and we chat amiably. Three minutes become ten, and finally the General arrives and nonchalantly delivers their tickets.

At 3:15 Old Boy rides up the escalator. The General drags the bag around to the other side of the pillar. Once the coast is clear, he's off to help Junior buy and deliver his last six tickets. I'm holding the bag again. It's been a long week. I find myself dozing off.

My eyes pop open to the sight of Junior.

"Where'd he go?" he asks.

"Down to find you."

"Where's the bag?"

I smile. "I'm sitting on it."

Ten minutes later the brothers are reunited behind the column, considering whether they should buy tickets Old Boy didn't pay for.

"Here's where we can try to take a shot," says Junior. "The question is, do you do it?"

"Would a wire hit on Sunday?" asks the General.

"Do we buy on credit?" asks Junior. "How is Old Boy planning logistically on handing out 120 tickets?"

It's not clear which way they'll go. The promise hangs in the air, and gradually the moment passes.

"How much did we lose?" asks the General, who then begins putting the debacle in a context they understand. "You lose $5,000 in Vegas, it's no big deal. Ten thousand and I'm an idiot." The General raps his fingers against his head. "Twenty thousand dollars is an extremely bad weekend."

It will take them days to sort it out. Did the tickets spike because of diehard Philly fans? Was it the late distribution of secondary tickets? They'll never know. After leafing through scribbled names and numbers on hotel notepads, envelopes, and ledgers, they close the books on Valentine's Day. They lost more than $64,000.

The brothers are laughing now, sitting by the bag when Junior puts it in perspective, clutching $5,000 in his hand. "Of course we can turn $60,000 of green into $60,000 of cardboard." Which is a marvelously poetic take on what they've been doing the past week—turning green paper into orange cardboard that will be worthless tomorrow.

Sometime after four p.m., barely more than two hours before kickoff, the General says Old Boy tried once more to hook him. On the street, he told the General his attorney would sign a contract saying he'll pay him for half a million dollars of tickets. But the General hopped in the man's car and asked how he knew Old Boy. The

JONATHAN LITTMAN

General says the man replied, "He's just a guy who's supposed to get me two tickets to the game."

Fittingly, as the General's Ram pulls out of the garage, the Stones' "Midnight Rambler" blares on the radio. The time is a little after five p.m. Our last image of the Adam's Mark is none other than Old Boy pacing on the corner, phone glued to his ear.

Minutes later, we're on the freeway, driving by the stadium, Sunshine and Dirty joking about the seats they sold to the game that will finally begin in just over an hour. "Can I have the line and total?" asks the General, putting a dime on the game with his bookie—a first-half parlay, taking Philly with four points and betting that the score at the half will be under 23. Dirty doesn't have a bookie, so the General lets him bet $100 too. Sunshine also calls his bookie and bets a nickel.

The Little General turns to me. "That was the biggest Super Bowl ever. Thirty-five hundred for get-ins." No one talks for a long time. The black Ram is gathering speed now as we motor down the freeway in the fading Florida light. The Little General checks his messages and plays one that just came in. Old Boy. "Please, please, call me. Help me. I'm going to be killed. Help me, help me, help me!"

THE MASTERS

Inside The World's Greatest Golf Tournament

"Somebody else might have told you, which I think is so cute, a couple of people, probably three that I know over the years, have been defrocked. And they don't write em a letter, saying you are no longer a member. They just clean out your locker. And you go out there and your locker is empty, and that's the end of it."

— THE SOUTHERN LADY

CRASHING AUGUSTA

I once shot 84 on a tough course, and like all duffers, dream that one day my wayward putts will drop effortlessly into one hole after another. Golf tempts us with the possible because perfection appears tantalizingly within reach, even for just a single hole, and that keeps us coming back after all the shanks and screams. We're fanatical by nature. Witness the hundreds of golf training gimmicks and videos and books we buy to improve our swings. But perhaps I'm more fanatical than some. I've flown cross-country in the faint hope that I might see, smell, hear and feel perfection in the presence of golf's masters in their house of worship.

I'm suffering from Masters madness. Against all advice and reason, I am standing outside the gates of the world's most exclusive golf tournament. Every reasonable person I know has told me it's absurd to attempt to attend this tournament if you're not a corporation, guest of a corporation, or happen to have several thousand extra dollars to blow. The fact I've gotten this far is itself a miracle. I've actually secured a crash pad—last night I slept like a baby on an air mattress on the screen porch of a little brick house I'm sharing with seven guys half a mile down Azalea. With the city snarled in traffic, it's ideally located and you can't beat the price: my share of the week's lodging, and golf cart (rented on impulse from a local) comes to a bargain $425.

But here's the rub. The badge, or tournament pass for the Masters, costs $3,500 to $5,000 or more, and is harder to come by than a Super Bowl ticket. Price alone does not convey the tournament's exclusivity. This is the Deep South, where "Yes, Suh!" fills the air like the pervasive scent of Magnolia blossoms. Northern principles do not apply.

Headed by Chairman Hootie Johnson, The National, as locals proudly call it, is defined by its own rules. When the thunderous drives of a certain gifted player began soaring over the sand trap on eighteen, The National backed up the trap and lengthened the hole. As for

Hootie's headline-grabbing preference for excluding the fairer sex. "Well, we've adopted a new policy," Hootie proclaimed during his annual Masters news conference. "We don't talk about club matters, period." That means, "at the point of a bayonet," he added flanked by a bevy of green-jacketed members. "I said we have a new policy. We don't talk about club matters, period." Which is a pretty good idea when your organization excludes all women and counts just two blacks as members, while wholeheartedly embracing billionaires (six) and the nation's richest, most powerful white men.

Hootie ain't kidding about those bayonets. The Masters is more than just a sporting event. Augustans may be proud of their golf, but they love telling tales about another popular Southern pastime—guns and violence. The one about the time long ago when "some blacks were shot" for having made the mistake of fishing in one of the course's creeks, or the time a drunken lunatic crashed the main gate, roared up famed Magnolia Avenue and at gunpoint took five hostages in the pro shop, demanding to see the visiting President Reagan. But most of all, practically everyone in town is itching to talk about Alan Caldwell, the well-liked native son, who in 1997, the year of Tiger's first Masters' triumph, became the local partner of a hospitality club directly across from Magnolia, took hundreds of thousands of dollars in advance from prospective customers for tournament passes and watched in horror as prices skyrocketed to an unheard of $11,000 a ticket. When he couldn't meet his obligations, he walked into his yard on the first night of the tournament and put a shotgun to his head.

Shotguns aside, I'm not paying $11,000, let alone $3,500. Nobody's about to ask me to join The National, nor do I have a chance in hell of getting onto the Masters' Patron list, a system of vetting fans that first began with the launch of the tournament in 1934 by the legendary co-founders Bobby Jones and the iron-willed Clifford Roberts. Masters Patrons receive an unheard of license in modern sport, lifetime tickets to an internationally celebrated event. Once christened a Patron, you receive the opportunity each April to purchase for a nominal fee, (not long ago it was $100, now it's $175) a Tournament or "series" badge that offers entry to the holder to the four days of competition. Early on, The National solicited the members of golf clubs within 225 miles of Augusta, but at first it was tough to find takers, given the Depression, and the fact that only the rich could take off weekdays to watch a golf tournament. Indeed, though the Patron list remained exclusive, (the working classes rarely belonged to golf clubs) down on Augusta's Broad Street they virtually gave away tickets to the Masters until television and Arnold Palmer made it a hit in the early 1960's.

Who are these Patrons? The National has turned its secrecy into an art form, and on this subject, like virtually all else, wisely remains mute. This much they say: in 1962 a formal Patron mailing list began, and by 1967 the tournament enjoyed its first sell out. Five years later the Patrons' list was closed, and by 1978 the waiting list grew so long that it too was shut, opened briefly again in 2000, but then shut once more. The Patron list is a brilliant method of guaranteeing control and standards of behavior. At the top of the list are the members, about 300 rich and connected men, (nearly all white) who enjoy the privilege of membership at the National. They are knights in this kingdom of golf, Chairman Hootie Johnson, their undisputed king. A long step down are those Patrons who, like vassals—their medieval counterparts—receive their badges as grants from a lord. That grant, given to tens of thousands of privileged golf fans, is a lifetime charter to walk the hallowed grounds for four days each April as long as they live—and as long as they remain in The National's good grace. Just as lords required faithfulness from their vassals, so too does The National demand its Patrons obey its ironclad rules. Every badge has a number and if you or anyone using your badge violates the conduct laid out by Jones and Roberts, your badge will be taken away forever.

The National clears many millions a year from souvenir sales and television revenue. The club promotes the nostalgic idea that its golf loving Patrons will share their badge with family and friends so that the roughly 40,000 daily attendees who come to see the tournament and buy souvenirs are a different group each day. Share is the operative term. Get caught selling your badge and you risk a hell hotter than August in Augusta—the lifetime loss of your badge. That's the party line, but fundamental economic forces and money will not be denied. The patron list, bolstered by The National's notorious vengeance for violators of its precious code, creates the ideal conditions for an absurdly overpriced ticket.

Corporations devour so many of the available Masters badges that it seems ludicrous for an ordinary golf enthusiast even to try to get one. But to my golf-addled mind, the clear financial hurdle only fires my competitive instincts. If you can do Europe on $100 a day, why not the Masters on the same budget?

The idea of a pilgrimage to Augusta has a dreamlike pull, like a Dodgers fan's fantasy of being able to step back in time to stroll Ebbets Field. Hundreds of thousands of baseball fans make an annual road trip for spring training, a wonderful excuse to spend a beer fueled week in sunny climes, watching ball players up close and closing down bars. The Masters—the first Major of the season—is like spring training and the World Series at once. How can a true fan resist?

In the 21st century why must The National block out the modern world and shut its gates to the young and the decidedly non-corporate? With roughly half the competitors of most PGA events, the Masters features only the best darn players in the world, on the best course imaginable. To see them practice, joke around and compete—why should this great stage be taken from us, the true fans, and be spirited away by soulless corporations and Patrons in thrall?

Why can't we just go?

MONDAY

My golf cart hums through the neighborhood of plain brick homes laced with rental signs, and begins the climb up Azalea Avenue, past neighbors holding handmade $20 parking signs, the modest structures giving way to steroid-pumped, freshly scrubbed corporate hospitality centers. A white-haired elderly lady directs cars to her sprawling front yard, while across the way dozens of American flags flutter over the massive American Corporate Events, complete with its own putting green. Cresting the hill, I pass the vast parking lot of the block long Whole Life Ministry, and to my left are the Executive Club and VIP

Partners. A giant Bud billboard looms, Sergio Garcia smiling, "This is your beer."

Suddenly a motorcycle cop zips toward me. "You fixin' to get a ticket?" he warns, lights flashing.

Zooming down past the hospitality centers, I swing into a yard belonging to a little old lady named Helen Johnson and talk my way past her $20 parking fee. Because her plain white house borders the monstrous corporate hospitality mansions, she hopes to sell it for half a million as a teardown, whereas the same house 200 feet away isn't worth more than $100,000. During the year, the corporate houses are empty. "It's not a neighborhood," says Johnson. "It's a ghost town."

Back up the hill at Masters Corner, where Azalea meets Washington, The National's main gate beckons. "Tickets! Anybody need tickets? Cold beer, Cold soda! Cold beer! Extras! Anybody got extras?" Day one of Masters' week, and all the essentials can be purchased on this corner. A slender black man hawks plastic badge holders and cigars, while high school girls sell bottled water for a buck, and every third person streaming down the sidewalk is doing the one- or two-fingered salute, signaling that they need tickets. A man in a soiled t-shirt with eyes of wood preaches the gospel through a bullhorn, his daughter wearing a dowdy frock, handing me the day's leaflet, a golf ball on the cover, the words on the first page, "Bad news # 1. You are a sinner."

Scalping is legal in Georgia, but somehow, not near The National gates. "You've got to be 2,600 feet from the property," says Ronald Strength, Sheriff of Richmond County, a law-and-order man to his bones who, I've been told, won't wear the same shirt again till he's worn the other 17 in his closet. Twenty-six hundred feet means the no-scalp zone extends half a mile from the gates of the National. "We're snatching em' up," he says of the scalpers. "We've got plainclothes guys working outside as well as uniforms. We seize a lot of tickets."

But the Sheriff's story doesn't match what's right before my eyes. Masters Corner, where Wash Ave. meets Azalea is a bustling scalper's bazaar, over fifty hustlers and Patrons wheeling and dealing in plain view of a laconic deputy leaning on his squad car.

Does the Sheriff really want to arrest locals? From what I see, they seem to be the scalpers most likely to sell to a cop (indiscrete selling, of course, is what gets you busted). Patrons with extras roam up and down the block looking to sell their $31 Monday tickets for $300 to $350 or more. Meanwhile, many hustlers are planning ahead. "Wednesdays? Anybody got Wednesdays?" they shout, looking to buy tickets to the popular par 3 tournament day after tomorrow.

The azalea-graced ticket is nothing if not a perishable commodity. It was worth more yesterday than today, and as the minutes tick by on Masters' Corner, you can literally hear the dollars drain out of it as surely as the sun rises. By 10:30 a.m., $300 slips to $250, fifteen minutes later $200, then it's like air rushing out of a balloon. A distraught mother wheels her handicapped daughter to the corner—the girls' head hanging limply. "Hold on half an hour," suggests a hustler, "and I'll give you a couple for free." Suddenly, a Patron appears, places a pair in the daughter's lap and wishes them a pleasant day, an act of random kindness that brings tears to mom's eyes.

A little after noon, any fool can buy a ticket for $40 to $60 from the dozens of hustlers wringing the last bucks out of the days' market. Which is exactly what The National doesn't want you to do. "Do not try to buy a ticket from anybody out there," warns the Sheriff. "That ticket could be stolen. And of course, you cannot get in with that ticket."

But what do I have to lose? I catch a Patron exiting the gates who has had his fill for the day and slap him a twenty.

"Drink it or toss it!" the security guards call out just a few strides from the main gate. I gulp down my water, the guard reminding me to have my ticket in my hand. The second security line nears and there's no turning back. What if the Sheriff is right? "If a ticket has been reported lost or stolen," he says, "Augusta National immediately voids that ticket and you would be stopped at the gate."

The full body scanner screams, the guard ordering me to spread. His wand rattles like an angry snake, and I'm directed to empty my pockets. My ticket is good, but the scan has detected my cell phone, and I'm forced to check it at a stand. Claim check in hand, I finally pass the last checkpoint. Just a few steps inside and an official gives me a scare, barking "Keep your ticket visible!"

Instinct and economy drives me past the mobbed, cavernous shopping pavilion, where countless Patrons will spend tens of millions on souvenirs this week, the only authorized time when official Masters memorabilia can be purchased. Walking by the majestic green-rimmed scoreboard, international flags fluttering above, I'm struck by the first truth of The National. More than a golf course, it resembles a park. Though surrounded by gates and guards, the course rolls down before me, overwhelming with its openness and stunning vistas. The guys in my house warned that the greens tilt with the whimsy of a rollercoaster and I'll find it "way more hilly than you see on TV." It's more perfect than I imagined—the rough better than the fairway on most courses, the fairways' glassy putting surfaces reminding me of pristine polo grounds, grass so endless and perfect it literally speaks of money.

But The National is no walk in the park. Everywhere you look and everywhere you don't, officials are watching, marshals, volunteers, the MiGs (Men in Green jackets), and the undercover agents of the Masters' police. Beware. Even if you've managed to outfox perimeter security, doom may await. "Before you step on that course, there is Augusta National signage everywhere about what you can take in," advises the Sheriff. "There really is no reason to say you didn't know I couldn't take a cell phone or a camera." And if you slip a cell phone in, he warns, "It would be seized. It would be a mistake." The Sheriff isn't kidding. I've already heard desperate tales of grown men pleading not to have badge numbers taken down after a cell phone was found in their possession. They take away a lot more than your phone.

How serious are they? On an isolated part of the course, I break into a trot to test the no running rule, and within seconds, a cart appears, a man saying, "What do you think you're doing?" Drop a cigarette butt and it's likely to be still burning when one of the Litter Boys – squadrons of teens in bright numbered yellow jumpsuits with green-inscribed caps – stabs it with his Litter Lance. Rules dominate. The rules throughout the course: "Quiet please. Autograph seeking beyond this point prohibited. Authorized Personnel Only..." And the rules printed on the back of my ticket: "All ANI and Tournament policies, signs, verbal instructions of Tournament Officials, and traditional customs of etiquette, decorum and behavior should be observed at all times. Protests of all types are forbidden...VIOLATION OF THESE POLICIES WILL SUBJECT THE TICKET HOLDER TO REMOVAL FROM THE GROUNDS AND TICKET PURCHASER TO THE PERMANENT LOSS OF CREDENTIAL (S)"

That language about "removal from the grounds" rings awfully true. Remember that story about a "black" man getting shot for fishing at The National? The year was 1976. Two teenagers and a child were fishing in Rae's creek in front of the twelfth. National security guard Charlie Young shot a twelve year old in the leg and arm, and two nineteen year olds—one in the chest, the other in the leg. They lived. The National claimed the pump action riot gun "was discharged, quite by accident."

Fishing accidents aside, order has its advantages at The National. Tidy concrete bathrooms strategically located about the grounds border on the sublime, and on the men's end at least, there are no lines. No stench of bodily excretions, lovely chemicals fill the air. "Please do not throw cigarettes, trash, etc., in the urinal," announces a sign, and amazingly, when I do relieve myself in the massive trough, I feel as if I'm driving a ball down one of the endlessly perfect fairways, not a cigarette butt in sight.

Everything works in harmony, and it is a Kafkaesque exercise to try to understand. Query the men aiming the GPS Shotlink ball-tracking equipment at the 13th green, and they reply, "We don't know what we're doing."

The same goes with two young women driving big carts with light blue caps and blue pants.

"What do you do?"

"All kinds of things," they sing in unison.

"What kinds of things would that be?"

They glance at one another and laugh nervously. "All kinds of things."

The National doesn't bend, doesn't talk. "Those are their rules," the Sheriff says. "No sir, when they set em' that's what they gonna' go by." Like so many in this city, the Sheriff admires The National's code of silence. "You will not get members talking. It doesn't happen. I gotta' respect that."

TUESDAY

By Tuesday, I feel I've got the hang of this place. Around 1 p.m., a departing Patron wants $20 for her ticket. "How about ten?" I venture, and hold firm, gaining entrance for the price of admittance to a Multiplex. By chance, that afternoon while ambling down 18, as if in a mirage, appears Jack Nicklaus and Tom Watson, the champions of my youth. Side by side they climb the steep incline, chatting and laughing, a sight that brings tears to my eyes. It's late enough that the gallery here consists of another fan, and a couple of marshals. Jack pulls out his stick, and swings smoothly, the applause by the green registering a worthy effort. The legends play act for the gallery, Nicklaus pockets his par, and strides off toward the clubhouse, so close I could touch him.

The southern plantation style clubhouse hugs the ground in an inviting way, its wide veranda and simple white colonnade opening onto the lawn that rolls toward the famous Big Oak Tree, the bucolic setting for dozens of media interviews over the decades. Jose Maria Olazabal and Arnold Palmer heartily shake, the singsong cadence of the ebullient Spaniard, "AR-Knee! AR-Knee!" This is off-limits to ordinary Patrons, of course, but a mother with two kids sneak inside the green rope and corner Palmer for a photo, Dad gushing, "This is the greatest golfer ever."

The secret of The National is that it's not about the golf. You can see many of these same fabulous players on great courses half a dozen times a year for $30 a day or less. The wise come to take in the setting and the past. The Masters is as much about famous men as it is about golf, and no member symbolizes the history and power of the place more than Dwight D. Eisenhower. It's the stories that lend the course and its buildings weight and stature, and you aren't getting your money's worth if you don't take the time to absorb at least a few of the Masters' myths. Talk to enough folks here and you will hear wonderful tales of Eisenhower. It is fact, for instance, that club founder Clifford Roberts kept a toothbrush and set of pajamas at the White House for his frequent visits to President Eisenhower. John Boone, the courtly co-owner of a major golf cart distributor here, and a frequent National guest, tells the Eisenhower tale best. "After it was getting dark, one of the members said, 'why don't we go out here and putt a little bit.' And we just walked out and the Eisenhower cabin is right there by the putting green."

One of the men commented on how Eisenhower was such a big part of The National. "The member said, 'John, most people don't realize that President Eisenhower was a member of this club before he became President.'"

"I said, 'No, I didn't know that.'"

It was dusk, and Boone thought he was in heaven. "Sitting out there, looking at the sun settin', looking down across the eighteenth green, out down by number 7 tee box and Amen's Corner, it just takes your breath away." The clubhouse glowed, the Big Oak Tree in stark silhouette.

"Yeah, he was a member here," the man continued in a quiet, understated manner. "'The story is it was decided while he was a member here that he was going to be our next president.'"

The member looked at Boone, gave a little wink and a smile, and that was it.

As the light fades, I fall away from the clubhouse, down the slope, drawn to the belly of the course, the distant hum pulling my eye to another National miracle, a squadron of mowers in perfect Navy bomber formation, clipping a fairway in a single pass.

"Time to leave the grounds, sir. Time to exit."

It's 6:30, official closing time on practice days. At first, I figure I'm done. Then I walk toward the Berckmans Road exit, and slowly drift out of the tide of Patrons and suddenly realize that I'm invisible, circling about in the middle of the course, deliciously extending my sojourn. The time is a quarter to seven. I've snuck under the radar, outstaying even the marshals, slipped into a time warp, virtually alone on one of the world's most storied golf courses. Without the crowd, it's easy to stroll and dream of Jones, Sarazen, Nelson and Hogan, half a century ago and more. Many a visitor has rhapsodized about the rainbow of azaleas and dogwoods that sparkle like precious stones around the thirteenth green, but I'm more drawn to the sculptural and elemental purity of Alister Mackenzie's majestic design, the rolling, contoured fairways, the elegant columns of pines, the bone white sand of the traps ethereal in the dying light.

There is an Oz-like quality about The National, and if you're plucky enough to stay beyond official closing, you may be struck by the rarest vision, the chance to peek behind the Wizard's curtain. During each day of the tournament some 40,000 people flood the grounds, but at this hour, less than a dozen Patrons remain, and I might as well be a member, ambling about the course as if it were mine.

I walk up to the undulating eleventh where no less than six playoffs have been decided, a man standing by himself at the ropes in awe, saying, "There sure is a lot of history on this hole." Up on the green, a masked man in a white suit pushes a wide sprayer on two wheels, a second masked man keeping the hose out of his path. A dark layer settles on the green. Though the course owes its brilliant foliage to the nursery that once covered these grounds, natural it is not. Over the years, The National has dyed its creeks and ponds for the cameras and put the azaleas on ice to time their blooms. My favorite story though comes from a friend of a member who once performed the iconic Masters job of painting the inside dirt edge of the holes white for TV.

It is nearly 7 o'clock when I make my way past Ike's colonial revival cabin just off the putting green that Ben Hogan first designed as a practice hole, the nineteenth as it were. Only a handful of people remain, and the remarkable peaceful aura leads me to another truth. The ultimate Masters experience is not the tournament but to burrow as far inside as possible. What would it be like to spend the night at The National? A woman who wishes to be known only as the Southern Lady, a woman whose family stretches back nine generations in Augusta, can give you the flavor. "You can stand in that place. You can look all around you and you don't see any neon signs. No Kentucky Fried. Nothing.

"It's like going back to the womb," she coos. "It's so protected. It's pretty swish I tell yah, somebody rushes out with a golf cart as you pull up, and they snatch out your suitcase and hang em' up. Why they would unpack for you if you want em to. The service is divine. These ole-timey black men waiting on you, most of them worked there for years. And they call you by name. And the cute thing is, every member, when he goes out there, his coat, his green coat is hanging in the closet."

But what few know is that even a member has to know his place amid the Byzantine rules, know that the green coat can be taken away. The Southern Lady tells the story of members who committed the error of trading access for money, a great trespass in a club where the members are multi-millionaires and billionaires. "Somebody else might have told you, which I think is so cute, a couple of people, probably three that I know over the years, have been defrocked," the Southern Lady says. "And they don't write em a letter, saying you are no longer a member," she smiles. "They just clean out your locker. And you go out there and your locker is empty, and that's the end of it."

On the practice green, two blonds watch a professional stroke the ball with a feathery touch. A marshal spies a black man and I watching, and gestures for us to move toward the exit, "It's time to go." We head out but can't help but notice the blonds are not getting the boot. As we pass by the clubhouse, for the first time I notice a prim white sign with color codes granting access to a far more exclusive world—black, blue, red, striped green, orange and green. The man and I shuffle out together, while the blonds continue watching. The black man shakes his head, "I wonder why he's kicking us out?"

WEDNESDAY

The air mattress on the screen porch is surprisingly comfy, and while my neighborhood is hardly upscale, just a half-mile away stands the main Azalea gate and my favorite grocery store. Within golf cart range, down Washington Ave. (the cops only shoo me away on Azalea) beckons my favorite watering hole, sprawled on a dirt lot, the ramshackle Rheinhardts Oyster Bar, not to mention Hooters, one of John Daly's sponsors, where Big John signs autographs in the afternoon, and has been known to get wild in the night.

One neighborhood does not a city make. In search of classier surroundings, I take the front seat of the biggest, plushest BMW imaginable with a true Southern blond whose pleasant face graces Augusta billboards. Gwen Fulcher Young is not only the Mayor's wife, she also happens to be a witty tour guide and one of Augusta's top realtors. We're headed up past the venerable Partridge Inn, once the site of a gala reception for President Harding, into what the locals call The Hill or Summerville, lovely oak and magnolia draped streets with near hundred-year-old homes with grand porches and cool breezes. Gwen rattles off the Masters prices of some classic mansions. One she rented for $30,000 with no tickets for five days, another for $32,000 for the week, still another for $37,000. "Here we don't put prices on the tickets," she explains "but if you have tickets clearly you're able to sell somebody the whole package because they don't have to worry about going out and gettin' em." Nor apparently does one have to worry about unsettling inquiries from The National. It's as if the whole city operates under an unspoken understanding. You'll rarely find a direct reference to the badge or its price in writing. When corporate guests arrive, the badges are there on the kitchen table. This is how they do it in Augusta.

Gwen suspects Summerville may be beyond my means, so she drives me to what she dubs the "Nouveau Riche" Westlake, where "fresh and clean" homes rent from $5,000 to $20,000 a week, and CBS Sports often rents an entire cul-de-sac. She takes me to a spacious 5-bedroom home bordering a golf course that her assistant rented to ten guys for $10,000. Just "a thousand apiece" she says, including clubhouse and golf privileges.

Gwen spices her tour with social commentary and she is not the sort of gal to hold back. "Here in the South, we like to be invited. We don't push our way in," she says of Martha Burke's ill-fated fight to admit women. "What is it that Groucho Marx said?" she continues. "'Who'd want to be a member of a club that'd let him in?' That's kind of how we thought about The National. If they didn't want a woman to be in, who'd want to be a member? And after all they've said about it, who'd want to be in there anyway?"

Zipping the cart up to the course each morning is the best way to start your Masters' day, feeling the breeze on your face, smelling the azaleas and dogwoods. Strangers wave at you when you drive a golf cart on the streets as if you're in a parade, and women strike up conversations. I shuttle the guys in the house up and down for kicks, greeting the locals directing cars onto their lawns, and even take the cart to do my grocery shopping.

On Wednesday, a little after noon, I swing into Helen's front yard, holding an offering of fresh strawberries and a slice of pie. "Where do you want me to put it?" I ask

Helen's eyes arch wryly. "Do you really want me to tell you?"

Wednesday is the par 3 Tournament, what many Patrons consider the best day to see the Masters. Not surprisingly it is the toughest practice round ticket, costing $400 in the morning. But by noon, people are streaming out, and shortly thereafter I pay a hustler $40, four dollars over face, my total cost for three days, $70.

Practice days offer up little miracles. Vijay Singh at the pristine range behind the clubhouse, standing next to two irons he's propped up against each other in a triangle that defies gravity, sweeping his arms and hips through his grand arch, blasting one ball after another towards the massive, distant green net. Gary Player playfully skipping a ball over the long glassy pond approaching sixteen, right onto the green, ten feet from the hole. Or trailing the top secret Pin Committee, a clutch of serious Good Old Boys if ever there was, huddling around green after green, trying line after line, in search of the perfect pin placement for tomorrow's opening round.

But there's no doubt my favorite miracle is the Masters par 3 Contest. Played around two lovely ponds on a quaint practice course south of the clubhouse, the par 3 Contest is that rare spectacle, a competition purely about fun. Children or wives caddy for the players, the jaunty Swede Jesper Parnevik striding by with his two darling little daughters in white caddy suits, dad wearing electric pink pants and a pink on black shirt suitable for clubbing, a bemused middle aged woman, remarking, "Is he a wrestler or a golfer?"

The National was wise to make it easier for foreign players to qualify, and not only because they dress better, and their wives are hot. They have a lot more fun than the serious, grey-slacked Americans. This is the place to get an autograph, the scenes at the crowd knotted tees and greens unraveling like impromptu comedy skits. On the final hole, Miguel Jimenez grabs a camera, plops on his belly directly before the tee-box and aims the lens. Masters champion Jose Maria Olazabal steps to the tee for the long iron over the water. The marshal frets, but there's no time to pull out the rulebook, as Olazabal draws back without even so much as a practice swing, smacking the ball over his friend's head eight feet from the pin.

Everything that is beautiful and spontaneous and pure about the Masters can be found on Wednesday or Tuesday or Monday, the days you can get in for $50 or less, snap photos, get autographs, see the golfers in their natural habitat, and walk till your legs ache and they finally order you out. The greatest Masters moment is to be virtually alone on the course, and that can only happen on the practice days. They say money can't buy you love. It can't buy you the Masters either.

THE TOURNAMENT

Thursday dawns and the rules abruptly change. The scalpers are all but gone from Washington Ave. From here on out the only way in is on a badge, and unless you're on the corporate dole or a Patron or friend of a Patron, it's going to cost you not ten or twenty or even two hundred bucks but thousands.

Are Masters Tournament rounds worth the price? The only way to answer that question is with eyes and ears and feet, and so to have a fair point of comparison, I dutifully volunteer for the task of traveling to Pinehurst, North Carolina, site of the U.S. Open. Four straight days I faithfully walk the fabled Pinehurst #2, an average of 8 hours, seven or more miles a day. My daily tickets hail from the owner of Augusta's popular French Market Grille and a hustler: from $75 to $105, all at or below face. I might have paid less—cardboard signs by the road say

$50, a fraction of the street cost of a Masters practice round.

Compared to the Masters, the Open is downright inclusive. What duffer doesn't love the Tin Cup fantasy that even a pro barely skirting by could duel world champions? The Open field is far larger than the Masters, enjoying the serendipity of crowd-pleasing late qualifying wildcards that the Masters' unusually tiny field shuts out—men like Jason Gore and New Zealand Maori Michael Campbell. The Open also enjoys more fans and less corporate types—families, youths, college kids, senior citizens, and yes, blacks.

There is something inviting about the laissez faire style of the Open. Security is so haphazard you can easily sneak in a camera or cell phone, both found in abundance within the grounds, not to mention walk in free by the main gate without a ticket. Woefully undermanned, you needn't worry about someone reminding you to keep your badge visible, or telling you to shut up, or to stop running. Then again, I find myself itching to tell the beer sodden assholes to "shut the f—k up!" or at least beg some official to halt the stampedes chasing the leaders. "I can't see a f—ing thing!" yells a drunken idiot, breaking branches in a tree he's clambered up to watch Tiger's climactic put on eighteen. At The National he might have been ordered down at gunpoint, certainly handcuffed and carted off, and I would have been the first to cheer.

Which is another way of saying that while you can experience great golf at the Open and a handful of top tournaments, all things equal, just about every real fan dreams of the Masters badge. Getting one isn't simply a question of money. The Sheriff may warn against buying on Washington Ave., but then again, the Sheriff may not look at this problem the same way you or I might (The National provides him a badge for helping out with security during the tournament). The Internet? It's a crapshoot. A few sites are legit but it's hard to know which are one-man sham operations run out of somebody's home that routinely rip off fans.

And there's the little matter of the fine print on the Masters badge: "Ticket(s) may not be sold or rented through/to ticket brokers, travel agents or scalpers." Interestingly this apparent prohibition against dealing with mainstream and underground sources of tickets does not apply to locals. It is the Augusta Catch 22. There's nothing in writing or Georgia law that says a Patron can't rent or sell his badge (as long as you're a half mile from the gates). Which gets us to rule one on badges, the flypaper in the Masters experience. The only sure way to get a badge that ain't likely to win you a chat with a deputy is to get tight with a local or know someone who can. Sure, you can pay just shy of two grand—in advance—for a dive motel room on Washington Ave., or pony up three to five grand for an ordinary Augustan house, but neither of these "budget" housing options will get you a sure thing badge. For that you've got to pony up real cash, and do business with respected locals, like say the folks at the Partridge Inn.

Drenched in history, celebrated for its magnolia-draped balconies and popular bar, the Partridge charges less than $125 a night in the off-season. During the Masters that price leaps several fold, to five to six thousand for the week. Oh the "Tournament Package" gets you lodging, breakfast, and shuttle to and from the course, but what it really gets you is a local source for a badge. As a gentleman at the hotel explains, "The locals that have access to the badges, they're not really selling them to you. They're renting them to you." And as he so aptly puts it, "They trust me."

In other words, to properly "rent" a badge you first need a reputable realtor and mortgage. Spending five grand on a hotel room may be the safest way for an out-of-towner to rent a badge with a clean chain of title. The folks at the Partridge will even help you navigate the confusing rental process (lock in prematurely and you'll likely pay $500 too much; too late and it may cost an extra grand or you might not secure one). Reserve your room by November and make "arrangements" through the hotel to rent your badge shortly after Christmas, and chances are you'll get a fair badge rental, say around $2,700, instead of $3,100 to $3,500 or more. Unless another Tiger bursts on the scene and it's anything like 1997, when Nike would pay any price, and the badge goes nuts, shooting up to ten or eleven thousand, and the guy who said he'd sell it to you for three grand leaves you in the lurch and you've gotta decide whether you really want it.

I've heard a lot of badge stories and they're all bad. The Sheriff's right. Buy a badge on Washington Ave., and you may have just paid thousands for a pink slip a deputy will hand you as receipt for your confiscated stolen badge. Hustlers sometimes walk in fans with real badges for a few hundred dollars, then release them inside like fish, sans badge. Don't fall for it. The Masters police will likely nail you in minutes and the interrogation will be unpleasant. Sunday afternoon is the only time you can safely get a day's badge relatively cheap, for three to five hundred, when early departing Patrons hold up their badges at Masters Corner and auction them off to the highest bidder.

If I were to cough up my own dough for the Masters, I'd phone Gwen and rent a house with eight guys, filling the hours between strolling the grounds with playing golf or poker or merry making at the local watering holes. I'd advise my buddies to share Thursday-Friday badges (about half the full four day tournament rate), because on the weekend the action is on the back nine, and you're most likely to be watching the back of people's heads. But

I wouldn't rent, lease or purchase a badge. Three days is a hell of a lot of walking and golf and spectacle, and there's such a thing as too much of a good thing, and I can think of other sporting events I'd spend thousands to attend. Then again, hardly anybody turns down a free badge, and as fate would have it, I know a guy who has a badge coming back early Thursday afternoon. As long as I bring it back intact, and don't get busted for misbehaving or cell phoning or other Patron malfeasance, I'm free to borrow this almighty slice of paper encased in plastic and walk the grounds.

On Thursday and Friday I discover firsthand that a golf tournament can be a lot of walking and waiting. On the ninth fairway Phil Mickelson checks his watch as his interminably slow playing partner checks the wind and instructs his caddy to step off the distance, which is a lot of steps and not terribly exciting. At the tenth tee, Phil removes his glove to eat a snack, then slips it back on before settling down to some serious ball juggling on his driver's clubface.

Phil is still juggling when I can stand no more and begin walking out along the first fairway where Tiger too waits. Hand on his bag, shifting to hand on hip, foot tucked behind the other. Conveying ease and power and confidence, though at the moment he's playing for shit. Only a few fans are out here, a black man and his teenaged son and perhaps half a dozen others. And then, suddenly, Woods swings as if he's chopping wood, harder than I'd imagine. The ball pops straight up and caroms down, hits the pin, and skids into the bunker.

Woods looks up at the darkening sky, as if seeking some golf god. His hand slowly pushes his cap back off his head. He turns and chucks his failed stick at his bag. And then it gets worse. A none-too-happy Tiger climbs in the trap and his ball flies out hard, punctuated by "Sh—!" Back fringe, a long way from the pin. He gets a good look and misses the put. Bogey—that should have been an easy bird.

At the second tee the crowd hushes, bodies pressing forward. Tiger draws the club back and then something horrible and strange happens. He swings wildly, all arms and muscle, like a relief pitcher struggling to hit a curveball. The club head smacks the ground first—the ball popping up like a girl tapping a softball to second base. A weird hush ripples through the crowd. Tiger duffed his drive! Swept into the stunned crowd, I walk along the ropes behind Tiger, following him to where his ball rests in the cart path, about 160 yards short of where it should be. He takes a drop, once, twice, till he gets it right. And then hits another crappy shot. It's an epiphany for a duffer such as myself. Even the greatest player in the world can play like crap.

The funny thing is that the very next day, after more rain, and a weather delay, I find myself wandering down the second hole, right at the cart path where Tiger found himself the previous afternoon after he duffed his shot. On the right side of the fairway sit a clump of marshals in yellow folding chairs, chewing cigars. By coincidence, when the delay lifts Tiger will be on the tee, just as I saw him yesterday. One of the marshals rises, removes his cigar and bellows across the fairway to the corresponding marshals.

"Hey boys! You boys may want to move when Tiger gets up to hit!"

The marshals howl, slapping one another. But before Tiger can prove them wrong, God comes over the loud speakers. "Dangerous weather is approaching...lightning... Play will not be resumed. We ask everyone to seek shelter and leave the grounds immediately."

The man next to me kicks the mud. "How beautiful is that! I had to cut a deal with my wife just to get out here!" I too am crestfallen, and I didn't even pay a nickel to get in. "Careful with the weather folks," a marshal says, guiding us toward the gates. "It's coming on."

Minutes before the rain begins to pelt the roof of my golf cart in thick drops, I walk by the clubhouse, noticing this time that each gate has a different color: black, blue, green, and so on. I've been wondering about this since the first time I saw the sign listing the access colors. Finally, I ask a man inside the ropes, drinking a glass of wine, what it all means, what color gets you everywhere at The National. He's well dressed, though by the color of his jacket obviously not a member, and he understands the irony, smiling as he answers with a single word, "Black."

My Masters road trip has come to an end. I have no interest in forking over nearly a thousand dollars for a day at The National, and there will be no early badge returns on the weekend. Late Saturday morning we settle up, my share of the $3,000 house rental, golf cart, and week's food bill coming to $505. Throw in a Masters shirt and cap, seventy dollars for practice rounds, and a dozen National sandwiches and my total hits $694, slightly over $99 per day, all inclusive, for a week at the world's most costly golf tournament.

That afternoon I hitch a ride to Atlanta, waving goodbye to Helen, and fly home. More than a few Patrons warned that on the weekend the gallery on the back nine chokes off the greens to the point where you can barely see the top competitors. Sunday, they admonished, is the day to "watch it on TV." So instead of spending a thousand on a badge, I spend a glorious morning on a pristine beach, dipping my toes in the Pacific, and late in the day, like tens of millions of other Americans, catch the final holes on television and witness yet another Masters miracle—Tiger's Nike emblazoned ball hanging on the lip for an eternity before dropping into the cup, wishing all the while I was there.

MANHOOD

Rites of Passage

"Ordinary people, simply doing their jobs and without any particular hostility on their part, can become agents in a terrible, destructive process."

— STANLEY MILGRAM

THE BASEMENT

They take the men down to the dank basement. The temperature hovers around 40 degrees, but as the night goes on it will get colder. Windows are missing, and the men can see their breath. Sewage has backed up; the concrete floor is covered with three inches of gray water strewn with cigarette butts, garbage and dark chunks. They ask the men questions, and when they don't like the answers, they make the men get down in the water.

Two nights later the men are taken down again. They order them up onto a bench and pass them a five-gallon bottle of water. When they don't like the men's answers, they order them to drink. And drink.

And to pour the bottle over their heads.

The water makes the men dizzy, the room taking on an eerily bright cast. The huge man rages and orders the fans turned up full blast. There will be no mercy in the basement tonight. The water, the questions, the water, the questions. One bottle is downed, then two, three, four—more than 20 gallons drunk or poured over the shivering bodies of the two men. They warn the men not to urinate, but the gallons must go somewhere, threatening to burst their swollen bladders and engorged stomachs. The men pee themselves, the warm waves of urine spilling down their legs, humiliation a small price to pay for the momentary respite from the cold. They retch up the water in long arcs, vomiting till they're ordered back up onto the bench and handed another bottle and another. Finally one of the tormentors has a different sort of question: "Did you know you could die from drinking too much water?"

The time is nearly four a.m. Wednesday, February 2, 2005. Down in the basement no one thinks twice about the Geneva Convention's ban on torture. This is not Guantanamo Bay or Afghanistan or a secret CIA prison in Eastern Europe. Mike Quintana and Matt Carrington are students at Chico State University, pledges at the Chi Tau fraternity. During the next hour, the tormentors, the men they hope to call brothers, will determine whether they live or die.

Wired into our frenetic, high-tech world, we find it easy to forget the origins of male rites of passage, to think only of their most recent incarnations: rituals passed down by sports teams, college fraternities or the Boy Scouts. But few traditions are more ancient than forcing a boy through painful tests of courage and will to shatter his adolescence. Bloody beatings, wounds that scar, harsh ordeals in the wild—for thousands of years these have been the ways a boy becomes a man.

Classic male initiations began by ripping the boy from his mother. As Alex Haley showed in *Roots*, boys of the Mandinka tribe were literally kidnapped, removed to a male camp, run through rites of hunting and fighting and then publicly circumcised. The myth of man carving his character and place in the world through dangerous, noble deeds has a timeless appeal. By the early 19th century, American men placed huge stock in proving their manhood before other males. What actually made a man, however, was somehow mysterious. "The reason why this or that man is fortunate is not to be told," wrote Ralph Waldo Emerson. "It lies in the man; that is all anybody can tell you about it."

Young men went west; they sought oil or gold, or they searched out a stage on which to prove their manliness. Matt and Mike went to Chico State. Over the years, the school has made a name for itself, earning notoriety in this magazine and others for its comely coeds and legendary party spirit.

Chico would seem the ultimate California university town, and it is true that the quaint old Western downtown is crowded with bars. But Chico is far closer to Oregon than Los Angeles, lodged in the sparsely populated northern corner of the state. General John Bidwell founded the city in 1860 and planted lovely trees of endless variety, which now tower over the wandering creek that ambles through the pleasant campus here. Snow occasionally blankets the foothills in winter, agriculture and mining are the region's big industries, and a few miles away, lonely stretches evoke New Mexico's high mountain desert. Sacramento, the closest city of note is more than two hours distant; San Francisco is three. Unless you happened to have grown up in this city of about 80,000, Chico is a long way from home.

Those fortunate enough to attend prestigious universities may find it easy to dismiss a young man who would choose Chico State and join a fraternity with a reputation like Chi Tau's. But the lives and character of the handful of youths in this drama reveal a far more complex reality. The fate of Matt Carrington and Mike Quintana rested on those who had most recently survived the ordeal, the pledges from the class just before, the junior actives. The logic—common not just to fraternities, but to other male-dominated places as well—is brutally simple. Those who have just endured the abuse get first crack at dishing it out, their authority unquestioned. They've got *bump*.

Jerry Lim proudly wore the title of pledge general, a fitting one, since he had served in the Air Force. Short and intelligent, Jerry had hauntingly bad luck. His father left when Jerry was a year old; his mother was suicidal. Jerry scored brilliantly on the SAT and was accepted by the University of California, Berkeley, but his mother pushed him to join the Air Force. Jerry hated the military, leaving after three years to enter UC Santa Barbara at the age of 21; he partied there and soon flunked out. One month after his mother killed herself Jerry moved to Chico and rushed frats for the free beer, only to discover he actually liked the guys at Chi Tau. In Spring 2004 he pledged, aspiring to be pledge master the next semester.

John Paul Fickes, a slight ethereal boy, spent a lonely first semester with his grandparents, 30 miles away in a rural hamlet. A soccer player in high school, John Paul didn't drink or think of himself as a typical frat guy but found friendship with some "really smart" Chi Tau guys. The holder of a 3.9 high school GPA, who adored theater and dreamed of studying law, John Paul was impressed that many in the frat were putting themselves through college. He pledged in Spring 2004. "They liked me," he said. "They thought I was a cool guy."

Mike Fernandez, a strapping kid with good grades, was another gifted athlete drawn to Chi Tau. His first night in Chico his roommate, Ken Dandy, took him to a Chi Tau party. Beers were being sold from a soda machine, three bands were jamming, and the house was packed with at least 500 people, girls lifting up their shirts and flashing. Ken fell for the frat, pledged that fall and soon became Chi Tau's president. He convinced Fernandez that the guys were cool, that pledging was the best decision he'd ever made. Ken, who was on the Chico debate team, could be pretty persuasive. Fernandez said he also couldn't help but notice that his roommate, a "chubby guy with a beard," was suddenly going to cocktail parties in a three-piece suit, "all these hot girls hanging off him."

Ken offered his friend an elaborate Chi Tau history: founded in 1939, the frat became affiliated with Delta Sigma Phi in 1955, and all the famous Chico guys were Delta Sigma. Except Fernandez knew his pal was laying it on thick. Chi Tau lost its national charter because of what Ken termed a "bad rap around school," and Fernandez was dubious of his friends' claim that we "can go back to Delta Sigma anytime we want." He made the Dean's list and was surprised to meet guys, who like himself, were "really into school, focused." The closer—what pushed him to pledge—was the Chi Tau rush party in February 2004. They called it the Snow Social and carted in bales of hay and truckloads of snow from nearby Butte Meadows. They built a ramp and slid down it on snowboards and toboggans. "Just ridiculous," said Fernandez of the blowout, during which he snuggled up to more than a few coeds. "The girl-to-guy ratio was three or four to one."

Finally, there was Gabe Maestretti—Gabby as his brothers affectionately called him—sumo-wrestler wide, topping 300 pounds, with a bowling-ball head. Gabe had wrestled in high school and played football till he blew out his knee. No dumb jock, he had acted in Twelfth Night and Macbeth. At Chico he played the part of the fun-loving pledge favorite, the jolly Falstaff. He majored in psychology, but partying took its toll. For two straight semesters he couldn't pull off C's, and in late 2004 Gabe flunked out, reduced to working as a bouncer down the street at the raucous Madison Bear Garden.

Matt Carrington's first choice of schools was UC Santa Barbara, but when his Chico acceptance letter arrived in the summer of 2004 and there was no word from Santa Barbara, he headed north. By August, he'd moved to Chico. Then, out of the blue, his Santa Barbara acceptance letter arrived, delayed by a computer error. Matt took it in stride, telling his mother he'd already begun preparing for the start of school, saying, "It's just meant to be."

The antithesis of the stereotypical frat boy, Matt was a polite, well-mannered young man, adored by his mother and extended family. He'd been taking psychology courses for fun but was good at math and well-organized and hoped to become an accountant. For the past two years he'd shared an apartment with his father, rekindling a lost bond. Rangy, with a long, earnest face and jet-black hair, Matt was athletic though never the sort to join school teams. He was shy, and perhaps that was why a close family friend suggested he take her room in a little house in Chico after she'd graduated. Matt's two female roommates found him achingly sweet and soon drew him out for living room study sessions lightened by episodes of *Friends*.

Through this family connection, Mike Quintana and Matt Carrington became pals. Matt's friend had asked Mike to look out for him. Whereas Matt was a bit awkward around girls, Mike had looks on his side: an easy, drowsy expression to match his tousled brown hair. He liked to party, and Matt couldn't believe the way he'd walk right up to some guy at a frat house, start talking to him and the next thing you know he was in and chatting up the chicks. Just like that, he dragged Matt around to a bunch of frats, decided Chi Tau was the one and invited his new friend along for the ride.

Matt said he was too busy, but Mike talked him into it, and soon the two were caught up in the fall pledge tradition: endless calisthenics, late-night runs to buy beer or pizza for the brothers, raising and lowering the flag in front of the frat, cleaning house, various and sundry humiliations. In late September they dipped down to southern California for the obligatory road trip with three fellow pledges. Mike's toughest task was to walk into a store in boxers, grab a beer out of the fridge, open it and ask, "Where's the Vaseline?" Matt had to swap shirts with a homeless man and make an appearance as a hooker in a miniskirt and heels on a crowded Los Angeles corner. As winter approached the number of pledges dwindled. One quit, another was tossed for fighting, and a third left school. Attrition brought the fall class of 2004 down to just Matt and Mike. Quick–witted and good-natured, Matt earned the moniker Super Pledge, but he confessed to his mom that he was exhausted and just wanted it to be over. As the holidays neared, word came down that their pledge was being held over. They'd have to wait until after winter break for Hell Week.

Joseph Web smacked two freshman in 1684 to become the first Harvard man expelled for hazing. The practice traces its origins to ancient Greece, where young scholars were often bloodied by wild pranks. In the Middle Ages, what was called *pennalism* involved beatings with books or frying pans, the forced drinking of urine, and public humiliation. University students had to suffer the abuse if they wanted to become professors or doctors, and Martin Luther famously advised, "You'll be subjected to hazing all your life."

Throughout the 19th century, freshman at major universities were forced to run errands for upperclassmen and serve as the butt of harsh practical jokes. "Fagging" was firmly ensconced at English public schools, with domination the rule; a younger student was a senior's fag—meaning he fetched food and drink—valet and whipping boy in one. Hazing gradually became more dangerous. One night in 1873, a Cornell pledge abandoned in the countryside plunged to his death in a gorge.

More than two students a year have died in hazing incidents over the past three decades. Highly publicized deaths and injuries have led more than 44 states to pass statutes to criminalize hazing. Although most fatalities have occurred within college fraternities and involved alcohol, hazing has become endemic on high school and college sports teams as well, and a flurry of illicit photos recently posted on badjocks.com has spawned investigations at several universities. A recent NCAA survey of more than 325,000 college athletes reported that the majority had been hazed and that 20 percent of those had been subjected to ritualized beatings, kidnapping, or abandonment.

Is this hazing brutal punishment or torture? Many assume torture requires interrogation, but that changed with the photos from Abu Ghraib prison in Iraq. There was a weird familiarity to those disturbing pictures. Except for their setting, a military prison, the images looked straight out of a fraternity, with the sadistic

　　　　　　　　JONATHAN LITTMAN

emphasis on nudity and sexual humiliation. Abuse rarely falls within neatly prescribed bounds. The incidents at Abu Ghraib resembled hazing, punishment, and torture all at once. The abuses and gross humiliations carried out there and at Guantanamo drove home an old truth: men have been torturing and committing sadistic actions since time immemorial.

Popular sociologists have recently reported on bullying by girls, labeling the perpetrators queen bees, with some researchers arguing that politically correct notion that violence is learned behavior. Girls, they say, can be just as nasty as boys. While it may be true that a handful of women helped humiliate prisoners at Abu Ghraib, throughout history the physical torture, beating, and killing of prisoners is nearly always performed or directed by men. Violent crime statistics worldwide belie the notion that, as a group, women are as brutal or antisocial as men. Whether in Detroit or a remote third world village, men perpetrate roughly 90 percent of violent acts. The interesting question is why some men and not others.

Late on the night of Sunday, January 30, 2005, Matt and Mike are taken down to the basement of the Chi Tau fraternity house, ankle-deep in the filthy stew. Graffiti is scrawled on the walls: the names and dates of pledge classes, phrases such as "Remember the slaves" and "It's only in the mind." The basement has a foul, musty stench.

Mike remembers how often he's seen members spit and piss here, but what he feels is the freezing cold, the winter air rushing in through the broken basement windows. General Lim's title would seem to put him in command, but it's really a mob scene, the cavernous underground room packed with abusive, screaming men. The night begins. The two are told to get facedown in the water, forefingers and thumbs pressed together in a triangle for delta push-ups. Football burpees and up-downs. Wall-sits. Down onto their backs, into the murky water, legs and arms up in the air.

"I'm a little cockroach," they must sing, the filthy water splashed in their faces. It's cold, and they're exhausted and humiliated. Toward the end, after a couple of members have become ugly drunks, Mike realizes Jerry Lim may be pledge general, but he's also the only one protecting them from the dicks.

The night ends at five a.m. Jerry lets them change out of their soiled, wet clothes, and they crawl behind the washer and drier into sleeping bags in a cement cubby. It's the sort of nook a homeless person might call home. The tiny basement window is shattered, and their corner is no bigger than a crawl space, crowded with pipes and the drier duct. They close their eyes, but there's no sleep.

After a warning from a plumber that the pledges could get hepatitis from the filthy water, they are granted a basement reprieve. Pledge Olympics is Monday's theme, and the night begins with games in the living room. Foreheads against the handle of a baseball bat, the pledges spin until they can barely stand. They swing at a flattened beer can. They might as well try to hit a fly. Up the stairs they run—three flights, 10, 20 times. Again and again. It's exhausting, but there's no cold, no sewer water, only a few members screaming in their face. Gradually the night morphs into an impromptu baseball game, the goal of exhausting and humiliating the pledges forgotten. Near dawn, Jerry, knowing his charges had a rough Sunday night, takes pity on them and lets the two clamber into his top bunk for a couple of hours of sleep.

General Lim orders the pledges down to the still-wet basement floor for delta pushups. It's Tuesday night, 11 p.m. He shouts out a refrain, and they repeat, "I will never make Jerry Lim look bad again!"

"Pledge position number one!" Jerry yells.

They fall into the push-up position.

"Down!"

They drop.

"Up!"

They rise, shouting, "I!"

On they go, one push-up for each letter in the refrain, pressing out 34.

Jerry is good and pissed. They've fucked up raising the flags, neglected to wear plastic bags on their shoes, and generally made him and the other junior actives look like pussies. The senior members have been giving Jerry grief all day, and he's had it. The pledge general is going to "wipe his hands clean" for the night. He's barely slept the past two nights and has class in the morning. He won't stay in charge for the entire night and won't hold back his fellow junior actives. Jerry Lim isn't going to be nice anymore.

"What's my delta alpha?"

"Sir, Long Duck Dong, sir."

Matt has memorized the Chi Tau blue book, the frat's bible, and snaps back correct answers, including the members' nicknames, or delta alphas, but Mike slips, and when he does, Jerry explodes. The pledges are ordered out of their shoes, socks and shirts, and stripped down to their blue jeans; the wind chill from the fans makes it feel barely above freezing. They are ordered to look only at a smelly old shoe that hangs directly before them from the rafters.

Into the pledge positions they go—dozens of delta push-ups, plenty of burpees, and thigh-shaking wall-sits. Hell Week embraces the interrogator's standard method of total mental and physical control. Pledges can eat only what they are given. The general hands the pledges an "apple" (an onion) to eat, chased down by a couple of "cookies" (two cloves of garlic).

It's nearing midnight. Across town in the university library, Mike Fernandez is finishing up his calculus homework when he gets a message on his cell phone. Ken Dandy, the upbeat Chi Tau president, has a news bulletin: "I just want you to know that Hell Week has started and you have now gained your full rights as a member. I highly encourage you to come over and use them."

Ken is a friend, but the call unsettles Fernandez. He hated his own initiation, the members yelling and shouting at him, making him feel worthless. He wondered what was wrong with these guys. How could they take such pleasure in these sadistic rites? He had promised himself that after he got through it he would not be like them.

The week of push-ups, shivering in pools of ice water, sleep deprivation—it all made Fernandez so ill that when it was finished he checked himself into the university clinic. The nurse returned with a policeman. Fernandez wouldn't talk. He might have wrestled for Chico State, but he knew if he ratted out his brothers half a dozen of them would beat the shit out of him.

Exactly why young men in groups bully others is something of a mystery. Jane Ireland, a forensic psychologist at the University of Central Lancashire, has investigated the phenomenon in dozens of U.K. prisons and thinks she has the answer. In a recent study of 1,253 inmates from 11 prisons, Ireland made the remarkable discovery that 71 percent of the so-called bullies were also victims.

The finding challenges current thinking about bullying in prisons and schools. The surprising conclusion of Ireland and fellow researcher John Archer: the majority of bullies are victims who bully for protection or status. Contrary to previous theories, the findings suggest victim-bullies do not display any unique personality or type, says Ireland. Instead, bullying is largely a function of survival. There is a Darwinian element to it, and in prison victims must bully or be doomed to spiraling abuse. "You can start as a victim, and make your way up to a bully-victim," she says. "By bullying someone you make yourself a little less vulnerable." The harsh prison environment starkly illuminates the social forces that transform a victim into a bully. At the bottom in the bullying hierarchy are the so-called lambs, the victims subjected to the most abuse. It is no coincidence that researchers label them with a term reflecting feminine vulnerability. The group Ireland terms reinforcers, "the men who often clap and cheer and encourage the action," stands in the middle.

Henchmen align themselves with a "bully with a lot of status, someone very aggressive," says Ireland. Interestingly, henchmen "more or less do the bullying." Indeed, one of the ironies of bullying is that the wolf, or pure bully, need not always directly bully. Henchmen carry out his orders.

A strong offense, it seems, is the best defense. "Aggression is a valuable behavior among younger male groups," says Ireland. "If you're quite aggressive, it actually protects you." At many fraternities—Chi Tau included— rites of initiation ensure that new recruits, not unlike new prisoners at a jail, are abused and victimized. By giving recently victimized pledges the title of junior actives and granting them unchallenged authority to harass the next pledge class, fraternities ritualize and encourage the transformation of victims into bullies. "The fraternity initiation highlights the dynamic nature of bullying," says Ireland. "It's not about a person's characteristics. It's the environment that drives the bullying. It's where you are."

That Tuesday, movie night as they call it, Mike Fernandez arrives in the basement just after 12. Rex Garnett, a Chi Tau brother, carries down an old TV, his Xbox, and some poker chips. He brings three electric fans, too. Trent Stiefvater, a junior active, joins him on the couch and starts counting out the chips. Fernandez throws his arm around Matt. "You all right, buddy? Ya wanna quit? Don't worry," he says.

"Sir, no, sir," Matt says.

"Knock that shit off," Fernandez says. "You don't have to call me sir."

"Yes you do!" shouts Jerry, who then heads up to the kitchen.

Fernandez glances at his cell phone. It's 12:50. Jerry returns with a full five-gallon jug of Alhambra water.

"Water makes pledges grow!" he growls.

Jerry hands the pledges the bottle and recites the drill: Balance on the bench with one leg raised, head between the rafters and no touching the house, and drink till you can't drink anymore. Then pass the bottle to your pledge brother.

"All right," Jerry says. "You have ten minutes to finish this jug."

The poker table faces the pledges; the players are Rex Garnett and junior actives Jerry Lim, Trent Stiefvater, and Rich Hirth. John Paul Fickes and Mike Fernandez watch the game and the slapstick Bernie Mac comedy *Mr. 3000* on the old TV. They sit on a lumpy couch and chairs, joined by a few older members and other brothers who come and go. Bare foot up, leaning on his pledge brother, Matt starts to drink. And drink. He passes the jug to Mike.

"Take one for the homies!" yells a member.

Mike hoists the bottle over his head, the icy water splashing down, soaking his pants.

Mike has never felt anything like this before. It's cold like when you stick your arm in a bucket of ice water, cold long after it stings and goes numb. With half the bottle finished, Mike notices the room brighten. He feels tipsy. If he spills just a little, Jerry and the others shout abuse.

They yell at them to drink more. And they taunt, "You better not piss yourself! Don't piss yourself."

Then there's Jerry coming in close, playing the good cop, whispering, "Go ahead. Everyone has done it. It's the best way to keep warm."

Mike fights the fullness in his bladder, but Matt keeps passing him the bottle. They've drunk or poured out nearly the entire thing, five full gallons.

Mike can't hold back anymore. "Sirs! Peeing! Sirs!

In our modern civilized world will most men intentionally inflict pain on others? Isn't that the dark realm of criminals and sadists, society's fringe? In 1961, Stanley Milgram, a young psychologist orchestrated a series of experiments at Yale to find out. His newspaper advertisement for one of these said he was investigating memory and learning. Recruits, both men and women, were divided into teacher and learner roles. The teachers recited a list of two-word pairs, and then the learners, each strapped into a miniature electric chair with electrodes attached to their arms, were read a word and attempted to remember its mate. The teacher punished the learner for errors by flipping an electric switch. The first shocks to the learner were minor, less than 20 volts: As the number of errors increased, the shocks became far more powerful, the subjects crying out in pain and even fearing for their life.

The majority of the teachers kept flipping the switch all the way up to 450-volt shocks. Twenty-five of the forty subjects, Milgram wrote, "obeyed the orders of the experimenter to the end, punishing the victim until they reached the most potent shock available on the generator." Of course, the shocks were a fiction, the learners—actors. But the teachers believed the elaborate electric panels, switches and electrodes were genuine. They thought the screams were real, and some believed the victims might even die by their hand. The fundamental lesson, wrote Milgram, was that "ordinary people, simply doing their jobs and without any particular hostility on their part, can become agents in a terrible, destructive process."

Mike figures the night must be nearly done. They can't possibly do this much longer. But Rich Hirth grabs the bottle, walks up to the kitchen, refills the container, carries it down and hands it back to the pledges.

"Water makes pledges grow."

Mike can't imagine drinking another sip. But Matt keeps drinking, and so does Mike. One question wrong and they're paying the price, drinking for 15 minutes. Two bottles are downed, and Mike is ready to walk right out the door. He asks his friend if he wants to quit, and Matt says no.

Trent Stiefvater hears Jerry shout, "You're messing up!" You're messing up!"

Trent is a hunter and scuba diver accustomed to cold. During his Hell Week he'd simply cupped a hand before his face and let the water run off, faking it. But Trent takes pride in the Chi Tau rituals. He has learned the bawdy songs. He cares. To his mind, his fakery proved his ingenuity, the power of his survival instinct. These pledges are simply messing up.

"Get your leg up!" he orders.

Mike raises his foot off the bench an inch.

Trent closes in on Mike's face. "That how far you think it should be?"

"Sir, yes, sir!"

The pledge lifts his leg higher and tumbles to the concrete.

This ritual has a dark undercurrent, something no one has dared to tell the pledges. Mike is the black sheep, and many members don't like him. They claim he has disrespected women at their parties. Fernandez went to the meetings and listened as the brothers spoke of their determination to get rid of this guy. Gabe, Mike's big brother, told Fernandez, "I fuckin' hate Mike. I want him out of this fraternity so bad." But it's not that simple. "The only way to really get rid of pledges," Fernandez said later, "is to weed them out through the hazing."

The ultimate answer to why men are prone to violence may lie in biology. Aggression gives males a rush. "It's not surprising that males like to engage in sex and win fights," says Ruth Wood, a neurobiologist at the University of Southern California. "When they do either of those things their testosterone levels go up significantly for a couple of hours." Wood has recently performed experiments demonstrating that hamsters will essentially self-administer massive doses of testosterone, not unlike a human steroid junkie.

If animals and men crave surges of testosterone, which helps to explain basic urges for aggression and sex, there's another factor. Sex is inexorable. In nature polygynous male animals—and yes, that's what a man is—fight their way to impregnating as many females as possible. "Overwhelmingly, the majority situation in mammals is one of polygyny, not monogamy," says David Barash, a biologist and professor of psychology at the University of Washington. Antler-crowned male elk and massive male elephant seals strive to be the most vicious and promiscuous harem masters possible. It's brutal head-to-head competition with few winners and lots of losers. "For every harem master who may succeed in impregnating as many as 30 elk," says Barash, "there are 29 angry, resentful, and rather violent bachelors."

Which is why in nature and in humanity we find not only harem masters but dominance hierarchies. Baboons and macaque monkeys are rigidly hierarchical, like fraternity brothers. Are young college men that different from elk and elephant seals fighting to win females? Only those males tough enough to survive the fraternity initiation gain access to the hundreds of sorority girls. "If I were a biologist setting up a study that would be most likely to evoke strong patterns of violence in men, it would be similar to a fraternity," says Barash. "It's a situation of male-male interaction. All these wannabe silverback male gorillas, and only a few of them will actually succeed."

The third bottle seems impossible; Mike's stomach feels bloated like a football. He takes a sip and suddenly turns to the trashcan and spews a seemingly endless stream of water laced with the thin remains of the pledge apple. Five minutes later Matt too vomits up water.

Mike feels drunk and disoriented, but they have to keep drinking and answering the questions because they want to make it through the night.

When, around 1:30 a.m., Fernandez comes back down with his frat brother Corey Williams, the scene is surreal. John Paul, the gentle, quiet junior active, seems "so into the ritual," Fernandez has said. He's yelling, lecturing the pledges on house history, "determined," said Fernandez, "to make men out of these guys." The night has turned the former lamb into a henchman.

Fernandez approaches the pledges just as they finish the third bottle. "I'm going to give you one piece of advice," he whispers. "Don't drink all that water. Spill it behind your neck if you have to."

Then Fernandez gives a wink only they can see and says loudly, "Guys, don't piss yourselves!"

At that, Fernandez looks up and sees Gabe stumble down the stairs.

"Hey, Gabby, what you been up to?" says Trent as Gabe tumbles onto the couch.

"I'm so drunk, I just want to pass out."

Just like that his eyes shut, and he's fair game. Trent shoves the butterball Gabe, Fernandez tugs on the giant's chin hair, and Carlos Abrille, the house manager, joins in. Wrestling is a favorite house diversion, Gabe usually flattening his brothers until they cry uncle. That's how he got his delta alpha, his nickname: during his Hell Week they made him roll over the other pledges, nicknaming him after a monster truck called Grave Digger. Now, like a pinned tag-team wrestler, Gabe roars out of his slumber and cries for help. Trent reaches into Carlos's pants and gives him a wedgie. Five minutes of roughhousing later, Gabe has once again crashed.

Twenty minutes afterward, Jerry loses a big hand in the poker game, throwing it in for the night. A little more water and the night will be done. Jerry announces that his first lieutenant, Gabe, is now in charge. But John Paul remarks that Gabe has passed out.

"You're in charge till Gabe wakes up," Jerry tells John Paul before leaving. "It's almost over."

So John Paul, a 19-year-old freshman who moved into the house two nights before, takes the helm. He orders the pledges to pour the water over their shivering bodies, figuring it's more painful to freeze.

The big guy stirs, hunched over on the couch, squinting and growling.

"Why the fuck aren't the fans going? J.P. turn on the fan! Why the fuck aren't the flags up?" Gabe bellows. "Hell Week and you're just fucking us over."

A few minutes later Fernandez returns after hanging out upstairs. Gabe stretches out a hand holding the now empty water bottle. "Mike," he says.

Fernandez asks, "How many times has it been filled up?"

"Don't fuckin' worry about it."

"Aren't they done already?"

"Don't fuckin' worry about it!" Gabe thunders. "Just go!"

Fernandez starts to argue. Then Gabe pulls the junior active trump card.

"Bump!"

Shit, Fernandez thinks as he takes the jug. You can't say anything back to *bump*.

Why water? Through the ages torturers have forced innumerable victims to drink water for the simple reason that it terrifies them with the overwhelming sense of drowning. During the Inquisition, torturers knew the amount should never exceed two gallons if the victim was to stay alive. Recently, the CIA has reportedly held terrorist suspects underwater, a procedure euphemistically termed waterboarding. Less known are the Category III interrogation techniques outlined in a once secret U.S. Army memorandum written in October 2001 to the commander of the joint task force at Guantanamo Bay. They are extreme methods of torture that required the approval of the commanding general: "exposure to cold weather or water (with appropriate medical monitoring)" and another standby of the Inquisition, the "use of a wet towel and dripping water to induce the misperception of suffocation."

Now on their fifth bottle, Mike tells Matt to pour the water into his mouth and let it spill to the floor, not in order to stop drinking but because it's so heavy.

"Don't fucking spill the water on my house!" Gabe screams.

Mike Fernandez and Corey Williams have come and gone again. Both worry about the pledges' safety, but ultimately Fernandez goes home and Corey heads back to his room. It's after three. By now Mike and Matt have each peed themselves half a dozen times and vomited water twice.

Grave Digger has a new question: "Did you know you could die from drinking too much water?"

"Sir, yes, sir!"

He orders them down into their lukewarm excretions— slowly, till their arms shake. They slap to the concrete. He makes them start over. When they can't do another push-up he orders them back up, making Mike hold the bottle while Matt drinks.

"You fuckups!" shouts Grave Digger.

Halfway through the fifth bottle, Corey returns. "Can I talk to them?" he asks.

Corey has Matt lower his leg and Mike put down the bottle. "The night's almost over," he says, telling them to just pour the water down their backs.

"Can I use the restroom?" asks Matt.

As Matt heads up the stairs, Gabe orders Mike to pick up the bottle. But as Corey tries to cool things down, the bottle slips from Mike's hands, smacks the bench and sprays Corey. Enraged, Gabe says they will pay for drenching a member, and a frustrated Corey leaves.

"You guys are doing push-ups!" shouts Gabe on Matt's return.

Grave Digger orders them down onto the concrete, taunting them. Matt is slow to get up, and John Paul notices he's pale.

Finally, the pledges nail four questions in a row. One more, John Paul says, and that's it for the night. Mike can end it right here.

"What was the date of Gabe's pledge class?" says John Paul.

"Spring 2002," offers Mike.

"You don't fucking know my pledge class!" Gabe hollers. "You're my little brother, and you don't fucking know my pledge class!"

Matt collapses after the first push-up, but the big man orders John Paul to hoist him up by his belt. With Grave Digger screaming, John Paul yanks Matt up by his britches. One more push-up, two more....

Down in the dark, cold basement for one more push-up, Matt collapses to the concrete in a seizure, flopping around like a fish, teeth clamped down like a bear trap.

JONATHAN LITTMAN

Mike sees his friend's eyes flash red and roll back in his head. A dazed John Paul watches Matt's hands curl up to his chest.

Gabe sits on the couch, staring in disbelief.

"Call an ambulance!" Mike yells. "He's having a seizure!"

Mike jams his fingers into his friend's mouth to stop him from biting his tongue, and screams. Gabe rolls off the couch, taking the fallen man's jaw in his great paws, prying it open just enough for Mike to extract his fingers. And just like that Matt's eyes shut as if someone is drawing the blinds. John Paul bolts up the stairs and pounds on Carlos' door, then remembers he left to get a burger. He shakes Jerry, but he won't wake up.

Downstairs Matt has gone limp and seems to be snoring, his head cradled in Gabe's lap.

Mike runs up to see if John Paul has called the ambulance. They meet on the first floor.

"What's going on?" John Paul asks.

The phone is in John Paul's hand. He has dialed 911. All he has to do is press the green button and help is on the way.

"Let's not jump," says Mike. "He passed out. He's snoring."

John Paul believes there's something seriously wrong, but it's four in the morning, and he doesn't want to believe the voice in the back of his head. He hits the red button, canceling the call.

Back down in the basement, Mike is crying, nearly hysterical as he sits by his unconscious pledge brother. Carlos returns from his burger run and coolly takes command. "Take some deep breaths," he orders. "Calm down."

Carlos starts talking about the EMTs in the frat who have handled similar crises. Mike listens to Carlos and Gabe. They're on top of it medically, in charge, as they've been in charge all night. Why would they lie? Carlos says they have to get Matt out of his wet clothes and rushes upstairs to get a blanket. John Paul looks dazed, and Mike throws himself down by Matt to help pull off his sodden pants. Matt has crapped himself, but Gabe isn't concerned, saying it's perfectly natural. Carlos returns with the blanket, and they wrap the fouled, naked pledge in it and a sleeping bag and carry him to the couch. Once they've got him settled, Mike runs upstairs to change into warm clothes.

Gabe asks John Paul if he's planning to go to class in the morning, and Matt blurts out, "Nooooo," his voice slurred, then lapses back into incoherent mumbling. He lifts himself slightly onto his side and vomits water.

As Mike returns, Gabe wraps a massive arm around him, sits him down on the stairs, and hands him the sweatshirt off his back. He tells him he has to calm down. He won't let anything bad happen to Matt.

Mike returns to his friend's side, and Carlos says he's been talking, which makes Mike feel better. Everything, it seems, is under control. A few minutes later Carlos goes upstairs to his room to turn on his TV and eat his double Western bacon cheeseburger with fries in bed.

Gabe and John Paul have been talking to Mike for the past hour about pledging, sharing amusing stories to pass the time. Mike is sitting by his friend's head to make sure he's okay, when suddenly he notices Matt has grown quiet. He puts his hand by Matt's mouth and feels the faintest of breaths. John Paul hears Matt hiccup once, twice. Mike puts his face by his lips.

"Oh my God," he says. "He's not breathing. Call an ambulance!"

John Paul powers on his phone, but he just hasn't got it in him to make the call. He runs upstairs and pounds on Carlos's door.

"Matt stopped breathing," he says, handing him the phone.

Carlos takes the phone and runs to the top of the basement stairs and looks down. He calls 911 at 5:02 a.m.

Mike tips Matt's head back on the couch, clears the phlegm from his mouth and blocks his nostrils. He can't get him flat enough, so he moves him to the concrete.

Mouth to mouth, Mike gives his friend two breaths every 15 seconds.

He's given Matt four breaths when he sees it: foam bubbling out of Matt's mouth, not blood red but lighter somehow, orange.

"Fuck!" Mike says, terrified. The orange foamy blood just won't stop. It starts coming out of Matt's nose.

Before Detective Greg Keeney of the Chico Police Department began down the steps to the basement, he felt the cold rushing up. At the bottom of the narrow concrete flight, a uniformed officer waved a flashlight beam, and Keeney's eyes slowly took in the graffiti scrawled on the walls, the names and dates of pledge classes. Into the maze of rooms Keeney walked, the concrete slab and ripped sheetrock walls spray painted with "Never give up" and "We own you." In one room, the detective found a handmade coffin attached to a hoist so it could be lowered into a sunken pool of water. He thought the place looked like a dungeon, like something he'd seen in a movie. But it was the phrase written repeatedly in neat Gothic print that gave him pause: "In the basement nobody can hear you scream."

Just after seven a.m. Detective Sergeant Rob Merrifield and Keeney brought the half-dozen frat brothers into the main room. Dangling from the ceiling were hundreds of wooden paddles, green with red lettering, each maybe a foot and a half long.

The first uniformed officers on the scene had collected the incident reports. "Tonight Matt and Mike where [sic] supposed to drink water in an uncomfortable position for several hours," read Jerry's brief statement. "They would be encouraged to urinate themselves, and the night would end with them taking a shower and going to sleep...." John Paul's account was more detailed and optimistic: "At approximately 3:45 Matt (a pledge) started going into convulsions.... He was warm to the touch. After about an hour on the couch Matt began puking up water. He became more and more coherent and at one time answered a question...." Carlos's statement never mentioned Matt's name: "At arrival I heard that he was physically unable to stand. Picked him up from the ground and put him on couch. He was able to talk and was coherent. There was no alcohol involved. The person at hand did push ups [sic] and drank water, approximately three to four gallons...."

Standing before the anxious Chi Tau fraternity brothers, Merrifield didn't waste words. "I hate to be the one to have to tell you this," he said. "Matt didn't make it."

Gabe growled and slammed his fist into the wall. Mike began crying. Merrifield waited for Gabe to stop punching the wall. "We need to find out what happened to him," he continued. "We need your cooperation. We ask that you come down to the police station."

Gabe told the cop who took his statement that he wasn't there when Matt collapsed. "I was talking to somebody," he said. "I went upstairs, and I came back down, and he was just on the ground and he was kind of freaking out a little bit.

"Whatever happened it looks like it's going, it's passing. And then I was talking to John Paul, I think, and all of a sudden he's not breathing. We looked down, and he's got his tongue out and he's biting and, like, he's just spitting up mucus. So we're like, 'What the hell?' So I looked at J.P. and I'm all, 'Go upstairs. Get Carlos, and call an ambulance!'

"I have my hand on his chest, and I'm all, 'Mike! You got to breathe for him. You've got to breathe for him, make sure he's breathing!'"

In another police interview room, Detective Keeney asked Mike if he was hungry and then went to see what he could scrounge up. A video camera was watching. Mike began absently biting his nails and then was struck by something he saw on his hands.

Keeney returned and slid over a doughnut on a napkin. Mike let out a long, anguished sigh, his eyes still on his nails and fists.

"His blood is still on my hands."

Dr. Thomas Resk, a forensic pathologist, unzipped the white body bag at Chico Funeral Home. Witnesses present for the autopsy included Detective Sergeant Merrifield and Detective Keeney. Resk logged the time as 9:05 a.m., February 3, and noted the subject's height and weight as 71 inches and 150 pounds, eyes brown. Time of death was 6:10 a.m. the previous day, the cause cardiac dysrhythmia, a fatal heart rhythm created by an electrolyte imbalance resulting from hyponatremia, or water intoxication. Resk opened the skull and found significant cerebral edema. Whereas a healthy brain has gyri, ridges of brain tissue, Resk noted a flattening of the cerebral gyri and a narrowing of the valleys between them, the cerebral sulci. The water Matt drank had swelled his brain tissue until it expanded like a balloon ready to burst, tight against his inner skull.

The pathologist's other main findings were pulmonary edema and vascular congestion of the lungs. The capillaries lining the alveolar spaces had ruptured, bleeding into the lungs, and forming a pink frothy fluid that flowed into the trachea and out of the mouth. Resk could only speculate how much water Matt had drunk of the roughly 27 gallons he and Mike went through in about four hours. Resk's review of the medical literature made clear a fact that, at the time, seemed counterintuitive to the police: drinking too much water can kill. Matt died because he was pushed to drink himself to death, just as another pledge may die of alcohol poisoning.

The medical literature cites examples of marathon runners who have died of water intoxication, drinking so much that they too decreased the concentrations of the electrolytes key to transmitting nerve impulses and contracting muscles. Indeed, at least one other pledge at another college had died from ingesting massive amounts of water. Drinking a large volume of water can dilute the levels of sodium and chloride in the body to the point at which the heart and brain can no longer function. Symptoms include vomiting, confusion and seizures. Matt was doing what he could to survive—urinating, defecating, vomiting. But his body couldn't possibly shed the excess water as fast as he was taking it in.

At 12:15 p.m., Resk completed his autopsy and shared his notes with Mike Ramsey, the District Attorney. The prosecutor wanted to know whether Matt might have lived had his brothers called 911 at four a.m., when he went into the seizure. Acting within the first sixty minutes can save a life; experts call it the critical hour. Resk knew that from the second Matt collapsed, his time was running out. Once dragged to the couch, the pathologist speculated, Matt was likely in a stupor, the condition that often precedes a coma. The pathologist told Ramsey there was no doubt that every minute counted. "They needed to call 911," Resk said. "He was a young, healthy kid. He was still breathing. I suspect he would have lived."

The media descended on Chi Tau. TV trucks lined up, cameras pointed at the frat nearly the whole day, and the story quickly went national: the *Los Angeles Times, Dateline, Good Morning America.* The fraternity held a meeting, its 40 members jammed into an apartment, tempers flaring. "It turned into a lot of name-calling and blaming," said Jerry. "They called us stupid for talking to the police. A lot were blaming others for not being there. It got ugly." Attorneys' numbers were handed out. As John Paul put it, "The older members told us to keep our mouths shut."

The Chico Police Department and the District Attorney's office continued their investigation despite the wall of silence. They faced a strange paradox. Kill somebody when you're driving a car while drunk, and you face a heavy felony manslaughter charge with a sentence of four to ten years. Torture a kid in a fraternity, and the law is on your side. Hazing is only a misdemeanor under the California Education Code, rarely resulting in sentences of more than 30 days.

But on March 3, 2005, Ramsey astutely married hazing with involuntary manslaughter to charge Carlos James De Villa Abrille, John Paul Fickes, Jerry Lim, and Gabe Maestretti with felonies that carried penalties of up to four years in prison and a $10,000 fine. Mike Fernandez, Rex Garnett, Richard Hirth, and Trent Stiefvater were charged only with hazing, with a maximum penalty of one year in jail. "We need to understand hazing is about power and control," Ramsey said at a press conference jammed with national media and broadcast live on Sacramento television. "It's about victimization."

Rex Garnett was the first domino to fall, agreeing to give a voluntary statement to the DA on April 28. Within days, Rex was harassed and threatened by other defendants. The pugnacious Ramsey warned the defense that things would "not go good" if the threats persisted. The prosecutor had lost a childhood friend to hazing, sucked away in a nearby river, and understood the open wound of Matt's death. In the weeks after the pledge died, detective Keeney had kept the victim's cell phone activated to preserve it as evidence and couldn't understand why it kept ringing, until he learned the sad truth: Matt's family was calling to hear his voice one more time.

When Ramsey learned that Mike Quintana, his main witness, would soon be abroad, studying in France, he arranged for a conditional examination to get Mike's testimony on videotape. Then the defense made a tactical error. It fought Ramsey's application of the Education Code, arguing that some of the defendants were not currently enrolled at the time of the incident, affording Ramsey an opportunity to submit a brief explaining how the hazing was not only dangerous to human life, but essentially torture. "One might comment that whoever uttered the infamous statement that some of the atrocities alleged to have occurred in the Abu Ghraib prison were no more than 'fraternity pranks' may have had the Chi Tau fraternity and its brothers in mind," the brief read.

In August, Judge Robert Glusman calmly noted in court that if he found Ramsey could not file under the Education Code, the prosecutor could probably bring torture charges. The sentence for a torture conviction is seven years to life. Gabe and his attorney appealed to the Carrington family for mercy. Fernandez decided to cooperate and got 30 days in county jail. Ramsey then pressed for guilty pleas with an unusual condition: the defendants had to recount their crimes to the media to publicize the dangers of hazing.

Late in the fall of 2005, at an emotional sentencing, the four main defendants entered felony manslaughter guilty pleas, and the punishment was meted out: one year for Gabe Maestretti, six months for John Paul Fickes and Jerry Lim, 90 days for Carlos Abrille. Pleading to misdemeanor hazing, Richard Hirth got 45 days, Trent Stiefvater a month. Gabe Maestretti would have to serve all of his 365 days—not a second off for good behavior.

Jail sentences and court-ordered public apologies are not the only means to mark the passing of a life. Some of the men jailed for Matt's death were angry. A few weeks after entering their pleas, the defendants consented to interviews with this magazine and *Dateline*. His handcuffs temporarily removed, with a guard by the door, Jerry Lim wondered why Matt didn't simply say, "I've had enough." Carlos Abrille bemoaned his discovery that the courage and manhood he sought in his fraternity were an illusion. "We're supposed to be a brotherhood, in tough times be there for each other," he said. "Whereas in this case everyone pretty much turned tail and saved face and ran out."

But those in the basement that cold February night didn't get far. "I really wish I'd stuck around and made sure it didn't happen," said a remorseful Mike Fernandez. "I wish I'd fought, like, tooth and nail and made sure they were okay." Barely filling out his prison issue jumpsuit, eyes filled with tears, John Paul Fickes said his crime taught him never to doubt his gut. If only he'd believed in himself. "I went along with them," he admitted. "That's the thing that hurts the most—the sorrow—knowing what Matt's parents have gone through."

Gabe Maestretti received the most jail time of anyone in the group, and the former high school ham seemed to enjoy his notoriety, the press interviews and television appearances. He said he remembered almost nothing of his role in Matt's death, and he was persuasive as long as you didn't read the detailed account he gave to police.

The men in the basement are haunted by what they've done. Often before bed, Gabe closes his eyes and sees visions of Matt. "It's always there if I don't clear my mind," he said just before the guards returned the handcuffs to his wrists and took him back to the Butte County jail. "I've got to focus on other things. Someone will say something and it will sound like him. I'll see him out of the corner of my eye."

Even today you can see Matt. In the front window of his mother's home hangs a nearly life-size poster of him. He is sorely missed. The morning of Matt's death, after the horror of seeing his bloodied corpse at the hospital, his mother crawled back into his unmade bed, smelling her son in the clothes left in a heap on the floor. On the tidy desk lay a single printed page listing the New Year's resolutions Matthew Carrington will never get a chance to achieve.

JUICE

Did they or didn't they?

*"So, I'm going to ask you, in the weeks and
months leading up to November 2000,
were you taking steroids?"*

— FEDERAL PROSECUTOR INTERROGATING
BARRY BONDS IN THE BALCO GRAND JURY.

THE PERSECUTION
OF BARRY BONDS

The time was 8:02 a.m., and I was the first person to walk into what in the next year or more will be the chamber where Barry Bonds will be either vindicated or convicted of lying to a federal grand jury. My eye was drawn to the grand dais behind which Judge Susan Illston would preside during the trial, a huge seal of the U.S. district court anchoring the wall, a U.S. flag to the side. The courtroom had wood paneling and a high ceiling. Courtroom 10 had no windows, just like the place Bonds will go if a jury finds him guilty.

Outside the San Francisco federal building that December 2007 morning, dozens of photographers mingled around satellite-TV trucks. A couple of women in bikinis shivered as they tried to take advantage of the scene to advertise the virtues of a vegan lifestyle. Gradually the reporters and lawyers filed into the courtroom for the main event. A dour courtroom artist in a black suit entered with her sketch pad, her pens and pencils hanging around her neck like bad jewelry.

About 8:30 a bald guy strode in from a side door, taking a seat in front. Jeff Novitzky, IRS agent and Barry Bonds's nemesis, wore a dark suit and looked straight ahead. A few minutes before nine Bonds made his entry. His dark suit was of a better cut than Novitzky's and hung easily off his broad shoulders. The baseball star chatted and joked with his lead attorney, Michael Rains. Bonds's legal team was big enough to fill an infield.

This was opening day for Bonds in his arraignment on federal perjury charges. He would not make every hearing during the next year, but when he did you could count on Novitzky being in the courtroom, watching his every move.

I had first heard of Novitzky five years before, in the summer of 2003, weeks before the government raid on Victor Conte, mastermind of the Bay Area Laboratory Cooperative (BALCO), the company suspected of distributing steroids to high-profile athletes, and Bonds's trainer, Greg Anderson. Only four lawmen were working the BALCO investigation at the time. That summer and fall I met and talked to three of them a few miles from where Bonds pumped iron and became a home-run legend. From the beginning, the story they told me, which I wrote for *Playboy* back in May of 2004 was markedly different from both the official government account and nearly all the books and countless articles that would be published on the steroid scandal.

In the years since, Novitzky has risen to lead a nationwide investigation focused mainly on prosecuting athletes who allegedly lied to him or a grand jury about their use of substances believed to give athletes an edge. The media have anointed him a hero. The New *York Times* called Novitzky "an unlikely contender for the role of the Eliot Ness of the steroids age."

Novitzky has been portrayed as a lonely, honest lawman dedicated to a worthy cause. He grabbed the spotlight by taking on Marion Jones, arguably the premier black female athlete of her generation, then Roger Clemens, the legendary pitcher, all the while relentlessly pursuing Bonds, baseball's greatest home-run hitter.

More than any other of Novitzky's targets, Bonds has been painted by the government and the media as a larger-than-life villain, a portrayal that has inspired hatred, condemnation and death threats. Few have noted that the white federal investigator and white prosecutors singled out a black man when they had equal if not greater cause to pursue then-Yankee Jason Giambi or any number of fairer-skinned stars.

This spring's perjury trial of Bonds—scheduled to begin in early March—promises to draw a carnival of television, print and Internet attention not seen since the first O.J. Simpson spectacle. Forgotten in this media orgy is that Barry Bonds is no O.J. No one was murdered. Nothing was stolen. No victim has been found. And Bonds may not have done anything particularly different from hundreds of other ballplayers.

How did allegations of cheating in sports rise to the level of a federal crime and become a subject considered so critical that everyone from President Bush to Senator John McCain wanted to cast a stone at Bonds? Why did whatever Barry Bonds, Roger Clemens and Marion Jones said (or didn't say) become worthy of a $50 million federal investigation? Why for more than half a decade did so many miss the hypocrisy and brutal irony of what may one day be looked upon as the biggest put-up job in all of sports?

I began reporting on this story before it made a single headline. By early 2004 I'd already done more than 60 interviews with dozens of sources and have since stayed in the game. In the past year and a half I've written nearly 50 stories for *Yahoo Sports* and *Playboy.com* on the latest twists and turns in the case. I have had the opportunity to review secret grand-jury testimony and files so that I can report critical facts about this case that have never been publicly uttered. I flew to the Clemens congressional hearing. I attended all the Bonds hearings and virtually all the BALCO trials. I also got to Victor Conte, the man who started the scandal rolling. Along the way, I learned an old lesson.

The passing of time can sometimes lend perspective, enabling us to see what has been in plain sight all along.

BALCO first entered the public eye on September 3, 2003, shortly before noon, when a covey of unmarked sedans surrounded Conte's small suite of offices just south of San Francisco International Airport. Agents armed with handguns and rifles rushed inside. The crowd of TV cameramen and reporters invited to the show had no problem identifying the lead agency. There were 18 IRS agents, three FDA agents, the managing director of the U.S. Anti-Doping Agency, two San Mateo drug task-force agents and two agents with the Department of Homeland Security.

BALCO consisted of Conte, his business partner, Jim Valente, and Valente's wife, Joyce. Novitzky would later testify in court that he first heard about Conte in the late 1980s when Conte's nutritional-supplements business started to take off, adding that when Jones's husband, shot-putter C.J. Hunter, tested positive for doping before the 2000 Olympics, "It sparked my interest." But this was years before any national criminal investigation of steroids in sports. Novitzky was an midlevel anonymous IRS agent. Why would something as unremarkable as a shot-putter testing positive for steroids spark his professional interest?

A talented high jumper who played college basketball, Novitzky had grown up not far from Bonds on the San Francisco peninsula. Bonds had long been both popular and controversial in the Bay Area. The ballplayer awed fans and filled stadiums, but many locals found him less a Hank Aaron than a modern-day Ty Cobb—his talent matched by his surly demeanor.

Novitzky seemed to take the superstar's cavalier treatment of the media and fans as a personal affront, and his raw comments about the legendary black baseball player made some colleagues uneasy. Novitzky never expressed irritation at Mark McGwire, Jose Canseco or the numerous other lighter-skinned pro athletes widely suspected of steroid use.

Before Jeff Novitzky, the IRS had no tradition of investigating steroids. Criminal IRS investigators have a well-defined function: to bring tax fraud perpetrators to justice. Novitzky testified in court that his interest in BALCO came about because of suspected money laundering.

As the saying goes, "Show me the money." Victor Conte's total income from sales of banned performance-enhancing drugs and consulting added up to less than $13,000 a year—a four-year total of no more than $50,000—a fraction of the IRS standard for a criminal tax case.

Top officials at the IRS or the Justice Department had to give the okay for Novitzky to morph into a star federal drug agent leading a national investigation. Given the IRS's shortcomings, that was a remarkable transformation. At an April 2001 congressional hearing, IRS commissioner Charles Rossotti was taken to task for not cracking down on hundreds of billions of dollars a year of criminal tax fraud. "I am worried the IRS is a dog that doesn't have a bark," said Senator Charles Grassley, the Iowa Republican who then headed the Senate Finance Committee. The phenomenon of Novitzky's IRS drug investigation struck federal prosecutors as unprecedented. Novitzky's search-warrant request was focused on a crime his agency had no authority to investigate: "Victor Conte Jr. and others are involved in a nationwide scheme to knowingly illegally distribute athletic performance-enhancing drugs...."

Behind the scenes, Novitzky was given the green light to recruit state and local drug investigators. In August 2002 he began reading Conte's e-mail and rummaging through his garbage, hunting for clues. By February 2003, through Novitzky's pressure, Iran White, an agent in San Jose's Bureau of Narcotics Enforcement, was brought in to go undercover. An African American skilled in the use of weapons and hand-to-hand combat, White was the go-to guy for the FBI and other agencies investigating major narcotics dealings in California. On April 17, 2003 White was given $300 to buy a six-month membership at Bonds's Burlingame gym. White knew Novitzky well. They had worked together on numerous cases in which the IRS was called in to take possession of financial records after a drug arrest. The undercover agent thought Novitzky's quest to nail Bonds bordered on an obsession, saying, "Jeff has never held back what he felt about Bonds." Another of the original four agents working on the case told me, "Novitzky hated Bonds."

Just weeks after White went undercover, he, Novitzky and the other two agents met at the San Jose federal building with the assistant U.S. attorney overseeing the case, Jeff Nedrow. Novitzky named the targets of the investigation: Bonds, Jason Giambi and other major leaguers. Working undercover, White was soon lifting weights with Bonds's trainer, Greg Anderson. By late May 2003 Novitzky was so thrilled that he boasted to the two task-force drug agents about his hope to participate in a book and become famous. White also overheard the conversation. "He envisioned congressional hearings, book deals and TV," said the lead task-force agent. "I was uncomfortable with that."

"It was turned into a publicity stunt," said the other task-force agent, who found the idea that the IRS agent hoped to become a celebrity or profit from the case to be a clear violation of the investigator's professional code. "We don't chase headlines."

Then in early June everything began to go wrong. White woke up paralyzed. He had suffered a stroke, possibly brought on by the brutal Bondsian workouts. His recovery took months. Novitzky, the man who put him in that gym, never called or visited him in the hospital.

With White out of the picture, Novitzky became a world unto himself. He rebuffed attempts by the San Mateo Drug Task Force to bring in another undercover agent. Requests to bring in the FBI or DEA to do phone wiretaps or recruit new undercover agents were rejected. What had begun as a joint federal, state and local investigation was fast becoming one controlled by a single man. The undercover operation, wiretaps and dumpster diving were about to give way to something never before seen in sports: a parade of high-profile athletes forced to speak about their drug use under penalty of perjury before the watchful of an IRS agent—Novitzky.

Long before Barry Bonds became entangled in the steroids scandal, it was widely known that professional baseball had engaged in an affair with the juice. A year and a half earlier Ken Caminiti told *Sports Illustrated* that steroids helped create his MVP season, when he hit a career-high .326 with 40 home runs. Caminiti reckoned 50 percent of big leaguers were on performance-enhancing drugs.

Back in 1998 the hulking six-foot-five, 250-pound Mark McGwire admitted he was taking androstenedione, a steroid precursor, during the year he eclipsed Roger Maris's single-season home-run record. Not only was there no outcry or federal indictment, officials within baseball didn't even bother to test for steroids until *2003*. The penalty for the first positive test was counseling—a farce compared with other sports (track and field banned first-time violators for up to two years). In 2003, 100 major leaguers tested positive for anabolic steroids, and experts believe the ease of beating the tests suggests that in fact several hundred others were likely using the drugs.

For years baseball had embraced and rewarded steroid abuse with outsized fame and ballooning multimillion-dollar contracts. That larger context seemed incongruous with the strategy the government appeared to be taking in grand-jury hearings.

The main criminal focus appeared to be finding the perfect scapegoat. Bonds seemed an ideal fall guy for a government bent on proving the moral wrong of steroids. In the fall of 2003, he was subpoenaed to appear before a grand jury. Lead Bonds attorney Mike Rains met prosecutor Jeff Nedrow in his San Jose office in advance of the ballplayer's appearance. Bonds was not the first to testify; others had done so and before testifying had been offered the chance to see documents containing the evidence against them. As Rains recalls, Nedrow proposed "the deal that Barry and I come down and look at documents a few days before Barry's grand-jury testimony." Rains said they shook hands on the agreement.

A week before that scheduled meeting Rains said the prosecutor left the following voice mail: "Why don't you come about two to three hours before the scheduled grand-jury appearance. We'll let you look at the documents then. I'll see you at 10 o'clock."

Rains and his driver arrived early on the morning of December 3, 2003 to pick up Bonds at his Hillsborough home. The next stop was a San Francisco police station more than a mile from the courthouse. The government wanted Novitzky to play chauffeur to Bonds on the day of his grand-jury testimony.

"Novitzky was in his federal car," said Rains. "Barry and I jumped into the car, and Novitzky said hi."

The IRS agent drove, Rains in front, Bonds in back. "Novitzky was fuming," recalled Rains. "He was all hot and bothered. Barry was saying, 'Mike, we can't trust these guys.'"

When the sedan arrived at the federal building, "Novitzky did this 20- to 30-second wait," said Rains. The cameras pushed in. Rains said Bonds started screaming at Novitzky, "Get this motherfucking car moving! This is fucking bullshit!"

Minutes later they rode the elevator to the 17th floor. Nedrow walked them into another room and introduced Rains to Ross Nadel, chief of the criminal division. Nedrow abruptly announced that Bonds would not be allowed to look at any documents. Rains was furious.

"You want him to testify at one p.m.," he said he told the prosecutors. "It's 10:30. You say we can't look at documents. We had an agreement."

Nadel said there had never been an agreement. Rains countered that he had Nedrow's voice mail advising him to have Bonds there at 10:30. "Do you think I came here at 10:30 to let Bonds swear at me for two and a half hours?" Rains said. "We got here early to look at the documents."

Bonds was not given the same opportunity offered to virtually every other athlete who gave grand-jury testimony: the chance to view the evidence against them before they testified. When Bonds' 149 page grand-jury transcript was finally made public, in early 2008, there was no doubt that the slugger was being asked about documents he'd never seen.

Rains said, "It was a perjury trap."

At 1:23 p.m., after waiting nearly three hours, Bonds was ushered into the grand-jury room. Nadel explained to the ballplayer that he was being ordered to testify "in the public interest" and that his testimony would not be used against him in any criminal case except a prosecution for perjury.

Nedrow, who dominated the questioning, was certainly enthusiastic. Armed with cryptic documents and evidence, he quizzed Bonds about scribbles on Greg Anderson's calendars and reported results of lab tests. But Nedrow's sentences rambled. He seemed unsure of himself. Even he was forced to admit he was not very good at asking questions.

"Yes. You are confusing," Bonds said after Nedrow acknowledged his shortcomings. "I'm telling you," said Bonds to the jury. "Is he confusing to you guys?"

PROSECUTOR: So, I'm going to ask you, in the weeks and months leading up to November 2000, were you taking steroids?

BONDS: No.

PROSECUTOR: Or anything like that?

What does "anything like" steroids mean? Say, creatine, which is legal? Or Andro (androstenedione), the milder legal (at the time) cousin of steroids, made famous when a reporter spotted a bottle of it in Mark McGwire's locker?

Why didn't the government simply ask, "In the year 2000 did you take something you knew to be an illegal steroid?"

Later critics would say the nearly three-hour interrogation revealed ample circumstantial evidence that the slugger took performance-enhancing substances, but that wasn't the issue. The point was whether he had knowingly taken illegal drugs and lied about it.

After Nedrow showed Bonds exhibits of substances that Anderson allegedly gave him, he asked again whether he took any steroids.

BONDS: Not that I know of.

NEDROW: What do you mean by "not that you know of"?

The baseball player pointed to exhibits of two substances Anderson had administered to him, a lotion called the Cream and a liquid called the Clear. These two substances were to become the key evidence against Bonds and the centerpiece of the prosecution. Judging by his response to Nedrow, it seemed Bonds had no idea what they were. "Because I have suspicions over those two items, right there," he said. He added that after the BALCO case broke, a few months before, he started thinking, What is this stuff?

Call Bonds clever, parsing his words, leaving himself an alibi. But that's what he's entitled to do. That sequence and others like it don't sound as though he was absolutely denying the use of banned drugs.

On October 16, 2003 Novitzky's investigation took a bizarre turn. Behind the scenes, unknown to the public, the Treasury Inspector General for Tax Administration (TIGTA) opened an investigation of none other than Novitzky and his fellow agents. Six hundred of the approximately $60,000 in cash seized from Anderson was missing. Neither Novitzky nor the other IRS agents implicated would cooperate with the TIGTA investigators without lawyers. Coincidentally, that very same day, Novitzky, under oath, gave his first testimony in the San Francisco grand jury about BALCO:

NEDROW: Okay, how many of the steroids and growth hormone, just approximately, like how much quantity did you find in the storage locker?

NOVITZKY: We found—I think it was three cardboard boxes, you know, standard-sized cardboard boxes full of stuff.

NEDROW: And to be clear on that, we're talking not about the Clear or the Cream but just traditional steroids that—

NOVITZKY: It was the Clear, the Cream, traditional steroids. We also found many other prescription drugs, prescription diet drugs, thyroid-hormone drugs, other oral steroids. It was like a pharmacy in there.

Before the close of his first day of testimony, Novitzky recounted his interview of Greg Anderson. The agent said Anderson acknowledged that he gave out steroids, but only to men he called "my little baseball players."

Novitzky said he and the other agents tossed out the names of a number of San Francisco Giants, and Anderson agreed that they were "little." Then, Novitzky said, they focused on the big guys:

"Is Gary Sheffield little?"
"No."

"Is Barry Bonds little?"

"No," Anderson said. "He's not little. I don't give anything to him."

Two months later, in his 2004 State of the Union address, President Bush told the nation about the importance of Novitzky's landmark steroids investigation:

> To help children make right choices they need good examples. Athletics play such an important role in our society, but, unfortunately, some in professional sports are not setting much of an example. The use of performance-enhancing drugs like steroids in all sports is dangerous, and it sends the wrong message— that there are shortcuts to accomplishment and that performance is more important than character. So tonight I call on team owners, union representatives, coaches and players to take the lead, to send the right signal, to get tough and to get rid of steroids now.

Hearing that declaration by the President one might imagine the BALCO investigation belonged up there with the fight against Al Qaeda. On February 12 at a press conference in the nation's capitol, Attorney General John Ashcroft, accompanied by IRS Commissioner Mark Everson, announced a massive 42-count indictment of

Victor Conte, Jim Valente, Greg Anderson and track coach Remi Korchemny. Everson said, "The investigation took shape when an IRS criminal investigator detected suspicious cash transactions on the part of Mr. Conte through a combination of traditional detective work and through the use of data housed in the Currency Banking Retrieval System, an anti–money laundering tool which tracks large movements of cash."

The media took the government account at face value. In March 2004 *San Francisco Chronicle* reporters Mark Fainaru-Wada and Lance Williams blew the scandal wide open: "San Francisco Giants slugger Barry Bonds, New York Yankees stars Jason Giambi and Gary Sheffield and three other major league baseball players received steroids from a Burlingame nutritional supplement lab, federal investigators were told." (Bonds maintains his innocence; Sheffield admitted taking the Clear unknowingly; Giambi admitted using performance-enhancing drugs.)

Senator McCain held well-publicized hearings. "Baseball is a national pastime," said then-fellow senator Joe Biden. "There is something simply un-American about this."

The political attention continued to strengthen the public's sense of Novitzky's character and his case. But behind the scenes, in grand-jury testimony that was sealed and thus kept secret from the press, his case was beginning to crack. During Novitzky's second grand-jury appearance, he admitted, shockingly, that the Clear, the now famous undetectable performance-enhancing substance at the center of the vast criminal probe, did not appear to be illegal or even a steroid under federal criminal law. Dr. Don Catlin of UCLA's Olympic Analytical Laboratory had decoded the mystery drug. It was THG, or tetrahydrogestrinone. Novitzky's statement on the Clear was a staggering admission that could infect the entire case against Bonds and other targets. Here's what he said:

NEDROW: What does Dr. Catlin say if asked the question, "Is it, though, actually an anabolic steroid?" What does he say to that?
NOVITZKY: What he said was, you know, there's two different standards you're looking at. Number one, there's the standard of sport. And he said, you know, the NFL, International Olympic Committee considers it, yes, it's a steroid. If an athlete tests positive for it, they're going to get sanctioned that they've taken a steroid.

He said it was another matter when looking at federal criminal law, and the problem that you run into there is there's a certain amount of steroids that are listed under criminal law that say, Hey, these substances are definitely steroids. And then there's a catchall phrase that says if it's not one of these substances, then if you can say pharmacologically or chemically related to testosterone, which in this case THG is, and you also have to show that it enhances muscle growth in human beings.

And that's the problem with THG, to which Dr. Catlin testified to the grand jury, "No studies show whether or not THG does, in fact, enhance muscle growth. For us to show beyond a reasonable doubt that it promotes muscle growth would be impossible at this time because there's never been any medical studies on it."

In other words, athletes who took the Clear were literally in the clear. They had not committed a crime. The drug could not be described as a steroid under federal law. Athletes were arguably not even lying if they'd taken it and then denied under oath that they'd taken a steroid. Taking the Clear was not illegal. Nor was taking human-growth hormone or erythropoietin, the endurance drug. Sure, they were banned by many sports and you needed a prescription for HGH or EPO, but that didn't mean it was a crime to use them.

Now let's turn to the Cream.

Conte had cleverly designed a diluted mixture of testosterone and a masking agent that would make the ratio of testosterone and epitestosterone in urine appear totally normal in doping tests, even if one were taking the Clear. The Cream was a mask for the Clear. It was not designed to function as an anabolic agent.

Was the Cream illegal? Conte claimed he had simply stretched his legal prescription for testosterone to create enough Cream for 17 athletes. He would famously call the Cream "baby food." Yes, it had testosterone in it but only a fraction of what millions of middle-aged American men take daily to regain their strength and virility.

By the fall of 2004 the criminal case against Victor Conte and the original BALCO defendants was beginning to falter. Novitzky had testified to the grand jury that he had seized three large cardboard boxes full of illegal drugs, describing it as "like a pharmacy in there." But this was a considerable exaggeration. As a drug raid, BALCO was a bust. As for Conte's personal storage locker, the contents of the three giant boxes in Novitzky's big-fish story would have fit in one shoebox. Conte had personal prescriptions for most of the drugs, and *The San Jose Mercury News* reported that the total value seized was less than $2,000, hardly an international drug ring.

There was another legal challenge. Conte alleged the authorities had never showed him a warrant on September 3 until hours after the search of his offices had been completed. His claim was supported by the detailed notes of the IRS agent who documented the search. There was also the question of a missing 53 minutes in the official report. Conte claims that between 4:30 p.m. and 5:23 p.m. that day, Novitzky vainly attempted to pressure him into wearing a wire and cooperating against implicated athletes. Nothing in Novitzky's detailed memorandum reflects that alleged interrogation. Wendy Bergland, the IRS agent responsible for taking comprehensive minute-by-minute notes (the memorandum of activity), recorded no entries for that entire 53-minute period. Nearly an hour totally unaccounted for.

These were no small errors and omissions. The logical course in massive federal drug investigations is to fashion an airtight case against the kingpin—in this case, Victor Conte—then force him to go to trial or require his full cooperation before granting a plea, thereby exposing his whole network—in this case athletes, coaches, owners and league officials. Conte's lawyers threw a wrench in the government's plan. They moved to dismiss the evidence gathered in the original search based on investigative misconduct. They alleged, among other things, that Novitzky forgot to serve the warrant.

A hearing was scheduled. Novitzky's credibility was on the line. In October 2004 he filed a sworn declaration in Judge Illston's court asserting that my original May 2004 *Playboy* article "falsely stated that agent White overheard me discussing getting a 'book deal' in connection with my involvement in this case. This is untrue. I have never had such a discussion with anyone and have never had any involvement with a 'book deal' in connection with this case or any other."

Rains deployed a detective to track down Iran White and learn the identity of the two San Mateo task-force agents who had also heard Novitzky talk about his hope to participate in a book deal. According to the *New York Times*, the lawmen talked to Rains and told him Novitzky had engaged in a host of improper, if not illegal, acts ranging from tipping off the media to the BALCO search to falsifying investigative reports and his plans to participate in a book or movie deal.

The government dragged its heels in turning over discovery to the defense, until finally Judge Illston ordered it to disclose the secret investigation of Novitzky to defense counsel by May 25, 2005. The government sent the full 150-page report by Federal Express on May 31. With a hearing set for June 7, Conte and his lawyers knew they had struck gold. If made public, the investigation of Novitzky could threaten his credibility and scuttle the government's chance to prosecute Bonds and the other key targets.

After spending a small fortune by calling 30 athletes to the grand jury, the prosecutors all but abandoned their case. Conte argues they never had a case to begin with. Like magic, his 42-count indictment was reduced to two counts—one charge for distributing steroids and one trumped-up charge of laundering $100, the rationale for IRS involvement.

Victor Conte was sentenced to four months in prison. Greg Anderson served just three months. Patrick Arnold, the chemist who made the Clear, received three months. The other two defendants—Valente and Korchemny— received probation.

For the next couple of years Novitzky got a pass from his true IRS duties. He traveled the country, catching athletes in alleged lies about drugs that may or may not have been illegal. The only individual to receive a serious jail term in the whole scandal was not a drug dealer or an athlete but a defense lawyer who violated a protective order to give a *San Francisco Chronicle* reporter grand-jury transcripts.

After all these years and millions of dollars spent exploring performance enhance in sports, it's worth considering what we've gained. The $600 is still missing. A Treasury report found, after a year investigating Novitzky and other IRS agents, that "solvability factors are not present and do not justify any continued investigation."

We did see all those tantalizing stories in the *Chronicle* that leaked the testimony of Bonds, Giambi, Sheffield and others. What we didn't see were those parts of the secret record the government preferred not to be made public: the missing money investigation, Novitzky's questionable conduct and his misleading grand-jury testimony.

The biggest omission of all, however, has been the systematic cover-up by baseball officials of steroid use in Major League Baseball. For years MLB never had any real drug testing. It was a sham because officials realized how many billions could be made on pumped-up ballplayers swatting it out of the park. We were fed what the government wanted us to hear: the $20 million Mitchell Report that trashed some more players and gave the executives paying the bill—Commissioner Bud Selig and company—insulation from the scandal. Selig wasn't completely off the hook. The Mitchell Report revealed that he and his colleagues failed to tell Congress that in 2004 testing had been suspended for six months for all the players who had tested positive the year before. The dopers had been given a free pass until September—the end of the season. The report also revealed that players were alerted to the resumption of testing.

Shortly after the publication of the Mitchell Report, MLB team owners unanimously voted to grant Selig a three-year extension on his contract, which, judging by his near $15 million 2005 salary, amounted to about a $50 million payoff, roughly the same price tag as the BALCO investigation. The president had called upon team owners and coaches to take the lead in cleaning up the sport, but the men in suits were protected by the government. Not a single baseball commissioner, owner, or manager was called before a grand jury.

The steroid scandal has been all about greed and power. Baseball is a multibillion-dollar business. The athletes are not innocents, but blaming the scandal on the gladiators overlooks who runs the Coliseum.

This past year Judge Illston, who presided over the steroid cases, indicated she thought the federal government's resources were being wasted. She sentenced the two latest individuals convicted in BALCO, the cyclist Tammy Thomas and track coach Trevor Graham, to home detention over the desperate objections of prosecutors.

At Graham's sentencing, she said pointedly, "I don't view sending Mr. Graham to prison as a useful exercise for this government at this time."

Barry Bonds is the next defendant in Judge Ilston's courtroom. Roger Clemens is thought to be on deck, accused of lying to Congress about taking human-growth hormone nearly a decade ago, a drug baseball didn't even bother to ban until 2005.

The show must go on.

POSTSCRIPT

On the eve of the Barry Bonds trial in the spring of 2009, the federal prosecutors lost their nerve and appealed one of Judge Illston's evidentiary rulings. Legal experts called it a Hail Mary pass, but perhaps it was something else, a way to back out of the collapse of a $50 million federal mistake. The appeal meant the trial was canceled. A year later in June of 2010, a federal appeals court in San Francisco affirmed Illston's ruling that BALCO drug tests and doping calendars were inadmissible. The trial is now scheduled for March of 2011.

In the year that the Bonds case was in limbo, several more top baseball stars have been revealed as less than candid about past steroid use. A-Rod, Sammy Sosa, David Ortiz and Manny Ramirez all said they'd never used steroids. Fortunately for them, they never said it to Jeff Novitzky. There has been no sign of any pending criminal investigations. Nor are these bit players. Ortiz and Ramirez helped the Red Sox win a pair of World Series titles in 2004 and 2007, and as the New York Daily News reported, A-Rod went from "steroid zero to World Series hero in just nine months."

The hypocrisy of the criminal prosecution of Bonds reached new heights in January of 2010. Mark McGwire revealed that he used steroids on and off for nearly a decade. A guilty conscience did not appear to be the motivation for the retired slugger's decade late confession. McGwire had been hired as a hitting coach with the St. Louis Cardinals, and his longtime manager, Tony La Russa ordered him to set the record straight.

No such luck for Barry Bonds. Baseball's all-time home run king lost a year or two at the end of his career because major league teams appear to have colluded in not offering him a contract.

In August of 2010 Roger Clemens was indicted for making false statements to Congress that he had never taken human-growth hormone or steroids. Novitzky left the IRS in the spring of 2008, and joined the FDA. At this writing he is investigating Lance Armstrong and the U.S. Postal cycling team on fraud charges related to alleged blood and performance doping that took place six to ten years ago.

BALCO The Sequel is gathering momentum.

SPEED

The Secrets of the World's
Fastest Men and Women

"Everything is clicking. It all feels effortless. It's going to 17 seconds, then 18. I could see the tenths. It's the Olympics. If I pull it, I pull it."

— MICHAEL JOHNSON ON HIS
WORLD RECORD, 200-METER SPRINT

THE PERFECT SPRINT

*T*wenty men line up in steaming hot Olympia shoulder to shoulder, Greek visions of male perfection: bottleneck waists, bulging thighs, and proud, muscled chests. The year is 164 B.C. Forty thousand frenzied spectators crowd the stadium embankments and surrounding hills.

The sprinters are magnificent, their tawny skin shimmering with a coat of olive oil. This is the stade—a straight shot the length of six hundred of Hercules' feet laid end-to-end—192 meters. The judge nods and the runners dig their toes into the staggered marble starting sills, one slightly ahead of the other, crouching like swimmers readying to dive. Taught ropes form a starting gate. The herald blows his trumpet and the starter shouts "apete!" and the barrier springs open.

Forty bare feet churn in the hard rolled sand, a wall of furious muscle driving down the broad track, "their naked forms gleaming upon the plain," one scribe wrote "so many arrows shot." The spectators roar, screaming wildly for Athenians, Spartans, and Alexandrians. But on this sweltering August day, one man is swifter than all, his feet light over the sand.

Leonidas of Rhodes is first to the final post. He wins the stade, the dialus, two lengths of the stade, and sprinting in armor with a shield. Crowned with the traditional olive wreath, the champion is showered with thousands of liters of fine olive oil, free meals, theater seats, statues, and lovers. Upon his triumphant return to Rhodes, the victor is honored by a parade of over a hundred chariots.

But even this legendary hero is mortal. As the years pass, Leonidas' speed finally begins to fade. Before his last victory is won, the quest among his rivals has already begun. Who will become the next World's Fastest Man?

Fog has given way to hazy sunshine this first day of November—opening practice in a new season for one of the greatest pools of genetically blessed athletes on the planet. The setting is the tattered West Los Angeles College track. By chance, the football field is crowded with more than one hundred men in prison-gray shirts trying out for the Los Angeles Avengers Arena Football League team. But no one would confuse these football players with the elegant creatures winding their way around the track. They walk the turn—a dozen men, a handful of women—and then take flight.

Hair flecked with grey, John Smith is a commanding coach. The tall, trim fifty-six-year-old moves with the pride of a man whose world record in the 440-yard dash is now in its 37th year. Though there is warmth in the lean contours of his brown face, his eyes can burn. Impeccably attired in fashionable athletic wear, Smith takes a seat on a ledge by the track under the shade of some pines, ministering to his fresh-faced sprint disciples. He gestures to the entrance. "When you walk through there, this is your Utopia. You are able to create whatever you want." He pauses. "Get through that one little gate. You got 400 meters to run around." He presses closer, "Your smallest focus is your greatest freedom."

It's hard not to gawk. Sheathed in thick sweats there's the rock hard Maurice Greene, the 2000 Olympic gold medalist, 2004 bronze medalist, and multiple World Champion. His head rolls playfully with his hips as he laughs heartily, joking with a teammate, a diamond stud flashing in his ear. Just as his sculpted body is a study in elegant proportions, powerful yet elegant, his face is classically shaped, with hooded eyes and high cheekbones. Greene smiles easily, and has a lazy eye, and moves with the sleepy, muscular sway of a lion. Tattooed on his bulging bicep is the biggest cat in the jungle and the initials G.O.A.T.—Greatest Of All Time. Already considered among the top two or three best sprinters in history, Greene is searching for one more Olympic triumph. Seven years straight Maurice Greene was ranked number one in the world. But Greene is 33. They say he is finished. He promises that he will prove the naysayers wrong at the Olympics.

This morning I am getting a chance to witness a rare thing in sport. Smith's troupe represents a radically different philosophy, an ongoing experiment, a team approach to the most individual of sports. Smith is the coach and spiritual center of H.S.I., also known as the Hudson and Smith Institute or Handling Speed Intelligently, a soup to nuts Southern California–based sports management firm headed by Smith and the agent Emmanuel Hudson, which trains and represents more than two dozen elite professional sprinters and hurdlers.

Smith's athletes have won at least 13 gold, 10 silver, and 10 bronze Olympic medals, and 14 world championships. Of the roughly 350 sub-ten second 100 meter performances in history, Smith has coached a quarter of them, over one hundred, and Greene alone has broken the vaunted barrier a phenomenal 52 times.

"Come on everybody!" Smith hollers, calling in the team, the hard work about to begin. The runners huddle, heads bent, palms piling on top of one another. The secret is in the eclectic mix. Here comes Leonard Scott, the barrel-chested former Pittsburg Steeler from Louisiana, a man with a stone hard jaw and look of quiet determination who recently clocked a swift 9.91 in the 100. The gracefully shy, eagle-like Torri Edwards, an elegant woman with a 100-meter world champion title on her resume. Hollywood-cool Willie Gault, the blazingly fast former Chicago Bear and sprint star, serves as a friend and mentor to these athletes. At 46, the amazing Gault can still keep pace with them in practice, demonstrating the value of dedication.

The sprinters release their hands and break the huddle, every one of them some shade of black. Smith and virtually every other sprint coach believe the fastest humans originate from West Africa. Studies have shown that they have far higher percentages of the muscle fibers necessary to sprint exceptionally fast. Just as the world's greatest long distance runners (East Africans) are blessed with high percentages of "red" slow twitch fibers, elite sprinters seem to have far greater percentages of "white" fast twitch fibers. Fast twitch muscle contracts faster and more forcefully. It's a gift of nature.

"Alright, let's go to work," growls Smith, describing the intensive skipping and high knee drills, 20 runs of 20 meters. These movements serve as the foundation for world-class performances. If a sprinter is dedicated, in a few years he or she may begin to master them and unlock the secrets of speed. You can't rush this journey. Perhaps more than any other element of the Smith method, these exercises are the indispensable first stage if you want to be fast. Along with the essential body position and movement, the drills teach the art of shifting smoothly, as Smith puts it, anticipating the "perfect clutch moment."

After the drills, they will run nine 100-meter turnarounds: striding a hundred, turning around, then striding another hundred. "That's the warm-up," Smith says with a cold smile, not mentioning the five fast 200-meter runs that will follow—the actual workout. "God Bless you."

They toe the line, eight lanes, two deep. Maurice Green commands the center lane, and with an imperial glance from side to side he takes the first group out. The

A skip features a high knee move in which the center of the foot strikes the track with force. Skipping doesn't capture it. Greene is a thoroughbred with the presence of a Baryshnikov. His calves reach out for the track and then hammer down with power and grace. The sprinters march in military precision, 16 feet striking the drum of the track.

The Greene movement does not come easily. Smith pounces on Leroy Dixon, the wide-eyed 23-year-old All-American, fresh from the University of South Carolina. Dixon has amazing bounce, but he's like a Slinky—all over the place. "You think you're getting it by reaching out for it," says Smith. "You're not. You're not taking advantage of this movement. The key is the dorsiflexed foot."

Smith pulls Dixon aside and shows him how to flex his foot, toes pulled towards the shin. Smith brings his foot down hard under him like a prancing horse, then back up underneath his buttocks. "You hit the ground like a spring board," he says.

The flexed foot maximizes forces and creates a wheel-like forward locomotion. Not strides so much as revolutions. The secret, Smith says, is the movement, the feet cycling in a circle. Pushing your foot back quickly as it strikes the ground—up and under and back down again.

"Arms back Leroy!" barks Smith. "Feel your movement."

The young sprinter glances at his coach, and Smith burrows in. "Pay attention to what you're doing. Put your chin down!"

Even for the supremely gifted, this is a challenge. Running in the shadow of Maurice Greene's uncanny rhythm and power doesn't make it any easier. My ankle stings, the start of a sprain.

We're on to the B skip—reaching with your calf and pulling it back fast under you. "Slow the drill down," says Smith. "Slow it down for the sake of everybody so we can get it right."

Suddenly, Smith shakes his head angrily. A couple of sprinters have eased up a stride short. He points to the red cones marking 20 meters.

"See this cone right here," he says, pointing a couple of feet short. Smith knows of one athlete who liked to stop his drills one stride short. "He wound up being number four all the time," he explains. "Nobody's fault but his."

If there's one American sprinter likely to take gold in Beijing, it's Jeremy Wariner. A Baylor University track prodigy, the 24-year-old runs the 400 meters and won the gold in Athens in 2004. Yet for all the attention he'll receive in the weeks leading up to the Olympics, the training regiment of a long sprinter is often a lonely exercise.

On a cloudy morning in Waco, Texas, Wariner's silver-haired coach, Clyde Hart, eases his new Cadillac through the main gate into a cemetery. The road is narrow and Hart winds through the tombstones and oaks, their leaves gold and red, pulling to a stop when the road straightens. Wariner climbs out, tall and all legs. He wears blue sweats and a yellow Adidas shirt, his skin pasty white.

He trots down the road and back, does a few gentle stretches, and then leans into the car to help his coach check his odometer. An easy workout on this early season day: Four 5 to 6 minute runs at a comfortable pace with two minutes rest between. Wariner slips off his sweats, and his legs extend, lean and sinewy, a human greyhound. Head shaven, face angular, he is built to sprint for longer than any other man. He clicks his watch and takes off through the cemetery as we roll behind in the car.

Wariner ruled the 400 meters the past few seasons, running in the mid to high 43-second range, and earning several million in endorsements and prize money. He's knocking on Michael Johnson's record of 43.18, and the track weenies are drooling on the Internet that he could Be the first white man to crack ten seconds in the 100. He's the first white American man to win an Olympic medal in the sprints since Michael Larrabee won the 400 in 1964.

Jeremy Wariner's first run is at a leisurely pace, and I join him on his second trot. He starts bounding down the road. Inches away, I can feel his float, the uncanny way he seems to fall into each stride. The first two hundred meters or so I hang by his side, needing three strides for his two, and then like a deer, he darts ahead and disappears among the tombstones.

Hart's Cadillac provides my locomotion for the next interval, and the coach takes me through his charge's lonely regime. Hart is old enough to have seen, and rejected just about every wacky new idea and gizmo that is supposed to make you fast. "They used to pull people behind cars. Now they have them put on parachutes," growls the coach, shaking his head. "It's busy work. You gotta run."

Simple running strength, Hart believes, has helped Wariner hold his speed longer in his races. In the fall, once a week Wariner runs 1,000 meters twice on grass with a several minute rest between. Each week he clips 50 meters off, cutting it to 950, 900... Another day he'll train like a miler focusing on aerobic conditioning—running sixteen 200 meters in 36 seconds, with two minutes rest in between. But Wariner doesn't want to be a miler. So each week he runs one less 200, but a second faster—15 runs in 35 seconds, then 14 in 34. "It's kind of like Pavlov's dog," Hart says. "He's going to run one less, but he's going to run faster. When the mind knows it's got one less, it's going to do that."

By summer Wariner sprints five 200s in 25 seconds. Another day he pops a few 350 meter intervals. "Go 40 seconds in a hard run and the by-product will be lactate—that's what makes the butt and legs heavy," Hart explains. "That's the essence of training. As the body learns to buffer this lactate, that's conditioning."

Wariner takes off on his last morning run, a cool down, and I join him. Hart let Wariner run a few national 200-meter races last year, and when I ask what he likes about the shorter race, he brightens. "It shows the speed a lot of people think I don't have. I know I can go under 20 flat," he says confidently. "The more I run it, the faster my time will be. And the good thing is it will get my 400 time down."

Wariner chats as if he were sitting at a Texas diner, ordering pie. My breathing grows heavy, and my questions come in labored chunks. "Track guys on the Internet...are saying...Jeremy...maybe could break 10 seconds... in the 100 meters."

He looks me in the eye, his voice light and excited. "It might be possible," he says. "I've never run a hundred before."

"What'd you do in the 200 last year?"

"20.19," he says proudly.

I nod impressed.

"So I know I can run a good 200."

Wariner is on the cusp of being fast enough to seriously contest international 200-meter races, something few white men have ever done. "Maybe one day Coach will let me run the 100, just to get a time in," he says, clearly excited by the prospect. "It could be a small meet."

We round a large tombstone, my breath coming in gulps. "What's the hardest part of the 400 for you?"

"Just staying mentally prepared for it. Just knowing I've got people on my back the whole time."

A couple more deep breaths and I ask the question anyone who's ever tried to sprint a lap would: "When you hit that wall in the 400, where do you feel it?"

Jeremy Wariner is not even breathing. "Honestly," he says. "I don't feel it anymore."

The single oval record Wariner hopes to break is owned by his friend and agent Michael Johnson. For nearly a decade Johnson dominated the 200 and 400, winning his first gold medal in a world championship in 1991 and his last in the 2000 Olympics. When we meet near his home in Marin County, California, Johnson doesn't hesitate when asked to name his favorite sprinter.

"Jesse Owens," he says. "He was a very efficient runner. He had incredible turnover, a great center of gravity. He was on top of his body." On the eve of the 1996 Atlanta Olympics, Owen's widow told Johnson that his straight up running style recalled her late husband. But analysts at the time thought different. "When I first came up," Johnson notes, "the television commentators would say, 'He has great talent. As soon as he starts to run the traditional way, he'll break a world record.'"

Johnson had been told he ran "funny" since he was a boy and started dusting kids in Dallas. College recruiters informed him they'd have to work on his technique. Johnson instead went with Clyde Hart, who didn't see much to change. But Johnson understands why so many questioned his style. The Jesse Owens model, the upright, rigid sprinter, had faded from the popular lexicon. "They did studies, though, and it turned out to be more efficient," says Johnson.

Quicker strides were the answer. It is a conclusion seconded by Ralph Mann, a renowned biomechanics expert who uses films of Johnson to demonstrate superior long sprint technique for USA Track & Field, the sport's governing body in America. Johnson, like Owens, proved small gears turning fast can get you there quicker than big slow gears. "It's the down force," Johnson says. "The harder you hit, the harder your foot comes down, the faster and quicker you're propelled forward."

The litmus test of Johnson's desire, mechanics and training was the 1996 Atlanta Games. No man had ever won the 200 and 400-meter races in the same Olympics. "I tried to point out all the pitfalls," says Hart. "I told him, 'You've never gotten an individual gold. You're the best 400 runner in the world. It's less chancy than the 200.'"

Johnson convinced his coach it was worth the risk. Pietro Mennea's world record of 19.72 in the 200 meters—set at high altitude—had stood for almost 17 years, much like Bob Beamon's miraculous near 30 foot long jump. The stage was set before the Games, when Johnson won the U.S. National championship in 19.66, breaking Mennea's mark. For the Atlanta Olympics, Nike designed him extra light spikes, the soles fashioned of carbon fiber, the feathery body woven with golden thread. He won the 400 by nearly a second. Three nights later, he lined up for the 200.

"I got a better start than normal, then I stumbled a bit," Johnson recalls. "When you get a good start gravity is pulling you down. You've got to pump your arms to keep your balance."

He didn't panic. "If you start to make too many changes you're out of the race." The first half of the 200 is a curve, centrifugal forces chewing up hundredths of a second. But Johnson came through the 100 in 10.12—sub-10 on a straight line. His quick, shorter strides helped. "I just was good at curves, always have been." Johnson made a smooth transition into the straightaway, not pressing too hard.

The dreamy euphoria of distance runners? "People always want to know what it's like," Johnson shrugs. "In the sprints, you don't have time to enjoy the scenery. You're executing a strategy." He felt the phases of the race like a Formula 1 driver shifting through the turns. "Everything is clicking. It all feels effortless." He's watching the clock as he nears the last 20 meters. "It's going to 17 seconds, then 18. I could see the tenths." With ten meters left, Johnson felt his hamstring go. A jolt, and then his leg wobbles. "It's the Olympics. If I pull it, I pull it."

The crowd erupted. The time—a stunning 19.32. Johnson had his historic double, cracking his own world record by a whopping third of a second. Topping 37 kilometers an hour, he'd covered roughly 34 feet a second. More amazing still, with a rolling start, Johnson clocked 9.20—in his second hundred meters.

Until that day there was no debate that the 100–meter champion had always been considered the all-out fastest.

But Johnson's last 100 of his record 200 meters was run at an average of 24.3 mph. or more than *thirty-five* and a half feet a second. The pundits started calling him The World's Fastest Man.

Coach Smith's genius is to approach the 100 as a long race. He breaks it into seven phases, starting with reaction time, that instinctive response to the starter's pistol. More critical is phase two, block clearance, the initial ballistic push—body low, chin tucked down, arms swinging up to the level of your head and all the way back. You set up the race with the drive phase, your torso and head gradually rising like a plane on the runway, accelerating the first 30 meters. Then comes the pivotal gearshift, phase four, the transition to overdrive—top speed. Too early, and it's like a jet taking off before it's built sufficient thrust. At 30 to 35 meters elite sprinters kick into phase five, accelerating till they hit maximum velocity around 55 to 65 meters. Maintenance is what Smith terms the next 20 to 25 meters, extending the max velocity. What's left? The final 15 to 20 meters, where, surprisingly, sprinters actually decelerate. Smith laughs, "I call that phase, 'Oh shit!'"

Moving smoothly through the subtle transitions in less than ten seconds is extraordinarily difficult. "I tend to jump out there and want to get it over and rush it and get tight," Leonard Scott confesses. "I get in a hurry. I get overanxious. I'm trying to get to the finish line and you're supposed to let the finish line come to you." Strangely, his coach says speed is not his problem. "Leonard has the first 60 meters down," explains Smith. "We're working on the last 40. His challenge is getting fit enough to run a 100 meters."

How can a runner tire in eight seconds? "Great sprinters generate huge amounts of rotary velocity," says biomechanics expert Ralph Mann. Elite male sprinters, says Mann, take five steps every second. "Try that standing still," he says, "let alone at 12 meters per second."

What happens inside the body? The gun fires and the sprinter drives his legs in a furious ballistic push, arms pumping. He burns fuel like a rocket engine propelling a spaceship into orbit. The explosive muscle contractions devour the small stores of energy in the cells, known as ATP (adenosine triphosphate). Within two seconds, the exhausted ATP is supplemented by creatine phosphate, but that energy store too is quickly depleted. Scientists dub ATP and creatine phosphate levels the phosphagen system—a six to eight second surge of energy. Once the sprinter runs low on ATP, he begins to slow. The slight deceleration is imperceptible to the human eye, but not to the timer counting hundredths of a second. How can you keep from decelerating? "The further into the race you can accelerate, the later you slow down," says Dr. Robert Vaughn, an expert in exercise physiology who heads training theory for USA track and field. "You have only about 20 meters of top speed. If that speed occurs deeper in the race you'll slow down later."

It sounds counterintuitive: to go faster, you must hold back your speed. But it isn't the only sprinting fundamental that has been radically updated in the last two decades. As recently as the late 1970's coaches told sprinters that the longer the stride, the better. Old sprint texts declared that the more time spent earthbound pushing, the better. But in the early 1980's Mann started showing coaches films and analysis that proved excessive ground time was the enemy. "They thought I was nuts," he says, but the film and computer analysis didn't lie. Great sprinters spend less then a tenth of a second on the ground for each stride. Mann's studies proved differences in airtime in elite sprinters were minimal. "It's how quickly you get off the ground."

When the sprinter's foot first hits it's actually breaking his fall. The talented sprinter quickly follows with a big "down push" generating 600 pounds of force as the ankle and foot come underneath his hips. What happens in the back? "The better sprinters shift everything toward the front," says Mann. "If you could physically do it, you'd never push off in back." What about that graceful forward lean? Except when accelerating and leaning at the tape, Mann says, "most of the great sprinters run straight up and down."

By the late 1980's most coaches had come around to Mann's thinking, focusing more on stride frequency than length, on increasing the sprinter's equivalent of RPMs. Smith and Mann have known each other since they competed in college. "He's a scientist," says Smith. "He bounces things off me and I bounce them off of him. He's helped me to quantify my assumptions. He'll sit down and explain how it works, why it works, and why it works faster." And of course Smith took the mechanics and physics out of the lab onto the track.

Smith likens sprinting to riding a bike. Just as there's an optimum air pressure for a bike tire, Smith aims for his runners to hit that "sweet spot" about six to six and a half inches in front of their center of mass. The perfect place to touch down is slightly behind the ball of your foot, "the spike plate behind the big toe," says Smith. "That's your power point."

Land in front of the ball of your foot, and "you're blocking, you're not round at the wheel," according to Smith. Strike flat-footed or on your heel and you'll rack up excessive ground time and generate less force.

Balance is critical. "Everything is round, everything is up under you. You can't flatten out." Nor can you tire. Mann's films and studies have proved man cannot run the 100 meters flat-out, and Smith's success has come in training his sprinters to maintain more of their speed in the final 15 to 20 meters. "You want to delay your max acceleration as far down the track as you can," Smith says. "If I can max at 65 meters instead of 58, I haven't used up all my energy. I'll have a better finish."

That precise calculus, shifting only when your body is ready, contrasts sharply with the warrior psyche of a sprinter, the mental games, the thundercloud of a race. Hundred meter men tend toward the wild.

"I'm like a lion in a cage just ready to come out," says Maurice Greene. "The beginning of the race is very intense: Pure power, pure intensity. Aggression."

Greene's story begins at the Third Street Church of God. Tall with red-and-brown bricks, it stands in a forgotten corner of Kansas City, Kansas. The projects lie at one end and across the street, a dismal stretch of empty weeded lots, broken up by a few homes fallen into disrepair. When night falls, dealers and prostitutes wave down cars, the background soundtrack of rap music sometimes broken by gunfire. This is where Greene first ran as a boy. Come the Sabbath he'd be in his Sunday best vying to be the second fastest kid on Third Street. "We were kids out there having fun, playing at Church gatherings, racing toward someone or going to the light pole," says Greene. "My brother Ernest was faster. He was older and had a lot of success. I just wanted to be better than him."

The elder Greene signed with Smith's HSI agency but chose to continue training in Kansas City. Though Ernest was faster and stronger, the younger Greene also burned up high school track—state champ in the 100, 200, and 400 three years straight. In 1995, Maurice Greene also signed with Smith, and like his older brother, stayed home to train under Al Hobson, the coach he'd had since the age of eight. After failing to make the 1996 national team and having to watch the Atlanta Olympics from the stands, Greene says, "I decided I had to leave Kansas." He saw what had happened to his brother. Wildly talented, Ernest Greene just hadn't made it. "My dad and I got in my GMC Jimmy, and we drove on out to L.A. I still remember my first day. It was September 26, 1996. I told Coach Smith, 'I want to put American Track and Field on my shoulders.'"

Smith had one question, "Are you ready to take everything I'm going to throw at you?'"

This was the off season, and Greene trained alongside Olympic 400 meter champion Quincy Watts from one to three p.m. at the UCLA track, where Smith coached. "It was very hard for me. He had me do the A skips, B skips, high knees. Everything is body position—how you strike the ground. How your arms swing. Your hands are your feet, your forearms your shins, your upper arm your thighs. I had to learn how to walk again. We would lift weights and then go out to the track. I would be very sore. The first time I threw up I heard them saying, 'We got one!'"

The arduous training left Greene literally too exhausted to step off the track, Smith often tossing a sweatshirt over him on the infield at three p.m. as the breeze kicked up. "I would be so tired. I would just lie there and sleep," says Greene. "Coach would start working out the college guys, and I would be just waking up when they'd be finishing at five."

Greene's Nike contract was a barebones $20,000, and he was so broke he slept on a friend's couch for two months. Even worse, he didn't seem to be getting any faster. "I was running meets, not even finishing in the top three. I was worried. Man is this going to happen? I gotta be a realist. What if I couldn't make it?" Greene started checking the classifieds for a job. "I went to the Prefontaine meet, ran 10.19, and took fifth. I was discouraged. Then I went to the

200. I was mad that I was in lane 8. I wasn't putting that much effort into it, and I looked over and saw I was in last place. Something clicked in me. I got the body position, ran everybody down and took 3rd."

The nationals were next. "Just before the race starts, Coach told me, 'You're about to run fast. Don't get too excited. Look at the time and take a deep breath and walk off like you knew you could do it.'"

"I ran 9.96 easy! I jogged in, thinking "Oh my God, what happened? I took my deep breath. Fireworks are going off inside. I'm thinking, 'I know how to do it. I can do it anytime I want now.'"

Greene did it again in the finals, winning in 9.9. He did it later that summer in Athens at the World Track and Field Championships, defeating the defending Olympic champion and world record holder Donovan Bailey. Twice more he would win world championships, once taking both the 100 and 200, a feat never before achieved in men's competition. He set world records in the 100 and 60 meters, the only man to ever hold both records simultaneously, and took gold in the 100 meters and 4X100-meter relay at the 2000 Sydney Olympics.

Barely more than a year later the Olympic gold medalist discovered his mortality. Riding down a freeway near Los Angeles on a motorcycle, he was sideswiped. The injury was potentially career ending: a broken fibula. Greene guarded the accident like a state secret, leaving the scene without even filing a police report. It was early 2002. Doctors kept him off his leg for a month, and then he began arduous pool workouts. Not until late April did he even step on a track. Smith didn't dare put him in a single meet before the nationals in late June. Miraculously, Greene won that year's U.S. championships in 9.88, but in rushing back he incurred nagging hamstring and quadriceps pulls. The tabloids in Britain dubbed him "Slo-Mo." Still in Athens, Greene nearly won back-to-back Olympic gold in the 100. Looking back, he believes a tactical error may have cost him victory. He eased up in the semifinal he was winning and took third. Relegated to an outside lane in the final, he says he "couldn't feel the inside of the race." Only two hundredths of a second separated his bronze from gold.

Leonard Scott slides his shoulders under a bar holding twice his weight. He squares his hips. The time is a little before 8 a.m., the place Gold's gym in Venice California. The air is thick with the sound of clanging iron and grunts and shouts. Looking down from the walls are images of a bulging Arnold Schwarzenegger, who trained here, and other monstrous Mr. Olympias.

"Straight from your feet!" commands Smith. "Now all the way up straight from the hips. Push the bar! Push it straight!"

For Leonard Scott, the man who would be champion, it's just another day at the office. His body shaking under the load, he rushes the next one. "You're trying to get out of it," smiles Smith wickedly. "Enjoy it!" One more brutal squat. "Let's go Leonard!" Smith barks. The sprinter drives the bar, legs wobbling.

Scott staggers out from under the bar. "My legs are gone," he wearily confesses. "We've been in the weight room every day this week. We've been running some crazy workouts: 400 (meters), 300, 200, 100." He shakes his head. "You come here in the weight room, squatting all this heavy weight. Then you have to go out and run, legs just dead."

Scott has reason to be tired. He was up at his usual 5:45 to shower, eat his oatmeal, and drive the hour and fifteen minutes to Gold's. In the two years since the 26-year-old quit pro football and fully dedicated himself to track, his body and fitness have been transformed. Smith has a nutritionist counsel his sprinters, and Scott has the enthusiasm of the converted. He dines often by six p.m., and is in bed before 10. He also makes certain to feed his muscles. Within minutes of his last morning sprint, Scott makes himself a protein drink right on the infield. "You have to put something in your body," he says. "You have micro-tears in your muscles. You have to rebuild those micro-tears." Lunch is a sandwich and salad, dinner, baked chicken or fish with vegetables. His weight has dropped from 195 to 183. "I'm lighter than I was in the NFL," he says. "But I'm stronger."

Squats and power cleans are his most critical lower body lifts, but the track is where he really works his legs. "A lot of people are amazed that we do weights early in the morning and then get on the track," says Scott. "Our legs are already tired, and we're trying to do a workout." The feeling is "almost like pulling the rubber band back," he says. "The weight feels like a heavy load." Then when the big meets come, says Scott. "He takes us out of the weight room. He lets that rubber band go."

Months have passed since I first endured a couple of painful days training with Smith's sprinters. They have been running intervals and bounding up hills. Once I joined them and had the gumption to trot beside Maurice Greene for fifty glorious meters and then sensed a power as raw as the ocean, what so many great competitors have felt, as we hit the hill and Greene shifted into second, then third, and blasted away as if I were a statue. This morning

I ask Greene how he's doing, and he shakes his head and smiles ruefully. "I had a little setback. A little minor injury," he says quietly. "My calf." He pauses.

"I wish as runners we would, like, tweak something in our arm," he laughs. "Because if we did that we could still run. It's always something with your calf or your hamstring. You can't run and then you lose a week and a half or two weeks, and it's hard getting back. I wish I'd be running, and 'Owww, my arm!'"

Greene tells me about the ultrasound, electrical stimulation, and massage he's been getting for his ailing calf, and then everyone gathers on the infield, stretching and jiving and spiking up, Smith making Torri Edwards blush, as he teases her about her attention-getting chartreuse body-hugging tights. Watching Leonard Scott shed his grey sweats and reveal his massive thighs and muscled torso, I think of how little separates good from great. Last year, Scott was ranked third in the world. If he holds or raises that ranking, you'll hear his name at the Olympics. If he slips a tenth of a second or sustains an injury, he'll be just another sprinter who didn't make it.

Greene is in the blocks, his palm raised like an axe, then chopping down as he fires off the line. In a minute, ESPN will go live with the first of three heats of the men's 100-meter dash at the 2007 Adidas Track Classic in Carson, California. Greene is cycling through his movement, little bursts that propel him halfway down the track. He walks back easily in his plain thick grey sweatshirt, stained with the sweat of his long warm-up. Veins bulge on his shaved head, and he rolls his shoulders. Today he is one of several Smith athletes in the 100 who will get ten seconds or so to prove whether they have it.

Greene's heat approaches, and the stadium announcer introduces the athletes: "Maurice Greene, 2000 gold medalist and 2004 bronze medalist. American record holder in 9.79."

The camera boom sweeps over the sprinters' heads, and a hush falls over the stadium. Greene is last to the line, last to settle into his blocks. The gun fires and this time it is not there. Not the start so much but thirty meters in. Greene moves to shift and can't find the gear. He trots the last twenty meters, looking as if he's trying not to pull a muscle, dead last.

I trail Greene as he talks to reporters, signs autographs for adoring kids, and then faces a tougher critic than the media, a finely sculpted knockout in heels and Capri pants who appears to be his girlfriend. "I couldn't," he shrugs, shaking his head. "I couldn't get out of the blocks. I can't get my tempo."

Greene heads into the crowd to the top of the stadium with the rest of his teammates who have finished their races or weren't scheduled to run. His crappy race all but forgotten, he enjoys the track meet with his friends.

The sleek, unflappable Torri Edwards is up in the 100. The gun fires and her start seems unremarkable. The first 10 meters she's no better than fourth. Her body still low, at 30 meters she calmly accelerates. Midway down the track her afterburner kicks in. Her confidence and control are uncanny, the poise of a dancer with piston-like synchronicity, everything they've been doing in practice the last six months, the whole Smith manifesto packed into this one race. You can feel it while you watch her. She's taking her sweet time, delaying her speed deeper into the race, and just like that she jets into the lead. Olympic gold medalist, Veronica Campbell closes hard, but Edwards dips first at the line, so fast she has to skitter over in front of her competitors to avoid barreling into the photographers.

Her time flashes on the big electronic board: 10.9, the fastest in the world this year for a woman, the best of Edwards' lifetime. She leaps joyously around the track. Greene hugs his teammates, jumping up and down, screaming. A performance this impressive means Edwards has a shot at Olympic gold, and Green is ecstatic, pointing at the spot 35 meters down the track where the race was won, where his teammate and friend won her perfect sprint.

"Did you see the gear she had right there!" Maurice Greene exclaims, eyes wide, turning to his teammates. "I knew it! I knew it!"

POSTSCRIPT

Time was not on Greene's side. A nagging calf injury sidelined him for most of the 2007 season, and in early 2008, with another season of grueling workouts on the horizon, Greene announced his retirement, his dream of a third Olympic 100-meter final dashed.

Torri Edward's impressive race at the Adidas Track Classic kicked off her best season in several years. She won the 100 meters at the 2007 Prefontaine Classic and the premiere international meets in France, Switzerland and Italy. She earned a number two world ranking heading into the Olympics.

Leonard Scott had double knee surgery to repair loose ligaments and then suffered a hamstring tear running indoors. He was a long shot to make the U.S. Olympic team. Rookie Leroy Dixon dropped his 100-meter time to 10.07, took two second-places in international meets and anchored the U.S. world championship 4X100 meter relay team in Osaka.

Jeremy Wariner continued his steady dominance, maintaining his number one world ranking in the 400 for the fourth straight year and winning the race at the 2007 world championships in his best time ever, 43.45—just 0.27 seconds behind Michael Johnson's world record. Then Wariner shocked the world of track and field by abruptly firing his longtime coach, Clyde Hart, and turning over his training to the respected but unheralded Baylor associate coach Michael Ford. Initial reports spoke of a contract dispute. Wariner took second at the Olympics to LaShawn Merritt.

In April of 2010, the Associated Press reported that "LaShawn Merritt tested positive for a banned substance used in an over-the-counter male enhancement product." Wariner recently apologized to Coach Hart, and is back training with him in Waco, Texas. In August of 2010, Wariner clocked the world's fastest time in the 400 meters for the year.

At the 2008 Beijing Olympics, Usain Bolt re-wrote the history books in the 100 and 200-meter dashes.

Michael Johnson's record of 43.18 in the 400-meters, set in 1999 in Seville, Spain, still stands.

Made in the USA
San Bernardino, CA
09 February 2015